The EARTH
HANDBOOK

Everyday Extraordinary

The EARTH HANDBOOK

Everyday Extraordinary

Christine McCartney
& Samantha Booth

THUNDER BAY
P·R·E·S·S

San Diego, California

THUNDER BAY
P · R · E · S · S

Thunder Bay Press
An imprint of Baker & Taylor Publishing Group
10350 Barnes Canyon Road
San Diego, CA 92121
www.thunderbaybooks.com

All notations of errors or omissions should be addressed to Thunder Bay Press,
Editorial Department, at the above address. All other correspondence (author
inquiries, permissions) concerning the content of this book should be
addressed to Saraband, Suite 202, 98 Woodlands Road, Glasgow G6 6HB, UK

ISBN-13: 978-1-60710-081-2
ISBN-10: 1-60710-081-9

Library of Congress Cataloging-in-Publication Data available upon request

Printed in China

1 2 3 4 5 13 12 11 10 09

Mixed Sources
Product group from well-managed
forests and other controlled sources
www.fsc.org Cert no. SGS-COC-004105
© 1996 Forest Stewardship Council
FSC

Contents

Natural Beauty

The Women's Environmental Network says that women use an average of 20 cosmetic and toiletry products in their daily cleaning and beautifying routine. Toothpaste, mouthwash, hand soap, facial wash, shower cream, deodorant, perfume—and that's just getting clean and smelling nice. We haven't even started on make-up!

Despite the natural-sounding names and pictures on the label, most of these products are a complex mix of chemicals, some of which are absorbed by the body and turn up in human fat tissue. Large quantities are washed down the drain into the water supply. The amount of resources that go into making, transporting and packaging cosmetics is also huge.

Of course, these are treats for many of us, and everyone enjoys looking and smelling nice. But why not clear out any products you never use, switch to certified organics where available and try cutting out just one of your daily beauty staples? Let's champion natural beauty and ease our impact on the planet's resources too.

January 31

Fun With Furniture

Can't stand the way that old table looks? Have stains and spills from people and pets made your sofa ugly? Before you rush out and buy new furniture, consider whether your old pieces can be refurbished. Old wooden furniture can be refinished or painted to give it a fresh look. Updating your sofa can be even easier; just find (or make) a new cover! As with electrical appliances (see January 7), refurbishing the old furniture rather than just buying something new may seem less convenient, but is better for the environment and your wallet. You'll create something unique, too, in an age where identical furniture from a handful of global brands turns up in so many homes.

Preserving furniture is good for the planet's future, but it can also be good for yours. Maintaining old furniture can have all sorts of emotional benefits. Years from now your grandchildren may be eating off that very same table. Or who knows—it could end up as a valuable antique! Either way, it's creative fun, and you will get years of use and enjoyment from the furniture and the memories that come with it.

"When we contemplate the whole globe as one great dewdrop, striped and dotted with continents and islands, flying through space with all other stars all singing and shining together as one, the whole universe appears as an infinite storm of beauty."

—*John Muir*

February
1

One Small Step for Teeth

Protecting the planet is a huge challenge, but thankfully there are also tiny changes to your daily routine that add up to a big difference. You'll hardly even notice!

Here's one of them. If you leave the water running while you brush your teeth, just stop from today. Turn it on only when you need to rinse, or better still use a glass of water.

If you do leave the water running while you brush your whites, over the course a week you will watch a whole bathtub of fresh, clean drinking water flow unused down the drain.

Water is becoming a scarce resource in many parts of the world, and it makes sense to save it where we can. A family of four cuts water use by something like an amazing 150 gallons a week with this step alone. If your water is metered, you'll save money by doing this, too.

Au Natural

- People have experimented with all kinds of alternatives to toothpaste over the years —options include coal, baking powder, sage leaves and table salt.

- If you aren't feeling that brave, why not try brushing with natural or organic toothpastes from your local health food store?

World Wetlands Day

Today marks the signing of the International Convention on Wetlands in 1971, to protect these very special ecosystems where water and land meet. A total of 6 percent of the world's surface is covered in wetlands, including shallow lakes, marshes, mangroves, mudflats, shorelines and peatlands.

These are vital for migrating birds, plant life and humans too—in many places they provide a livelihood and help to protect against flooding. But wetlands are under threat—the total area of wetlands on the Earth's surface has halved since 1900.

The southern Australian city of Geelong and Nagoya in Japan have been twinned by their bird populations for years, as they migrate between the two. Now the humans have caught up, connecting these two world-class wetland sites with a webcam project, so you can watch rare Australian and Japanese birds bobbing about at all hours of the day and night on your computer.

Visit their website or take a real-live trip to your local wetland spot to join in with world wetlands day yourself.

February
3

The Best Baby Food

When babies start to eat solids, their digestive systems are fragile. Many parents worry that they are more vulnerable to the nasties in our food, like additives and pesticide residues.

Making your own baby food from certified organic ingredients is the best way to be sure they are getting all the natural goodness without artificial colors, flavors, preservatives or chemicals. You can also set them on the road to healthy eating for life by introducing variety and using fresh ingredients.

Research shows that organic foods can be more nutritious. Organic full-fat milk, for example, is a great option for your children, with higher vitamin content and more omega 3 fatty acids than regular milk.

It doesn't take nearly as much time as you think to make your baby real food, especially if you prepare in bulk and freeze in baby-sized portions. Plus, it's cheaper, reduces packaging and saves on transport.

If you don't feel confident, invest in a baby cookbook (it makes a useful and unusual present for new parents who already have everything!) or check out recipes online.

Go Green at Work

Given how much time we spend with our colleagues, the workplace is a great place to make a difference and encourage green innovations. No one wants to be the office's green bore—the trick is to be positive and show how the changes benefit the company too.

There are lots of sound business arguments for cutting waste and increasing efficiency—beginning with saving money. Companies care about their image, and action on the environment will make a good news story. If you work in the public sector or for a charity, make the case that caring about the environment goes hand in hand with its ethos.

The way forward depends on your work situation. If you're home-based—great, you don't need to persuade others to get on board. If you are part of a big multinational, it might take longer.

Use whatever employee-feedback mechanisms exist to make constructive suggestions. Start with your own team and something simple, like cutting paper use. An environmental policy will include energy, water use, waste, recycling, sourcing and transport.

Check out Friends of the Earth for more greening tips.

February 5

WE RECYCLE

Sort It!

Recycling is the starting point for many green wannabes, but we often don't get around to doing all we could. It's time to set up a system, making it easy for us and those we live with to recycle more.

Firstly, find out what you can recycle in your area. Your local authority may collect some things (check online), but also try charities and businesses. Environmental groups and green stores may point you in the right direction.

Next, organize storage. You'll need a container for glass, plastic, textiles, cans and paper. Don't forget second-hand stuff needing a good home and space for small items like batteries and stamps.

Have a separate place for reusable things, so all your glass containers don't get smashed in the bottle bank.

Lastly, get your family or housemates on board with the new regime. Clean, rinsed and sorted items are much easier and more efficient to recycle, and they produce better recycled products.

Did You Know?

- Paper is one of the easiest products to recycle, and doing so saves energy and trees and stops rotting paper in landfill giving off greenhouse gases.

- Yesterday's newspapers can be pulped and back on the news-stand in just seven days.

- Buy recycled toilet paper; it's made from recycled paper (not recycled toilet paper!).

Everyday Vintage

We used to get a fabulous big bag of clothes every so often from our older, more fashionable cousins and it felt like winning the lottery. These deliveries are great clothes-swapping parties for kids.

It used to be the habit, but now families don't always live close and some people feel awkward about offering second-hand goods to others. But it's time to reclaim this splendid tradition.

Passing on outgrown clothes, toys and other children's things to others in the family or friends builds community and offers a very practical helping hand to parents you know. It also extends the lifespan of the items reused, cutting waste and saving money. And let's face it, some children grow so fast that they barely get to wear their clothes, never mind wear them out.

Hand-me-downs aren't just for kids, and if you have outgrown your own clothes, that trampoline in the shed or your old disco vinyls, offer them around to friends.

See also February 21 for details of Freecycle, and see January 3 for tips on clothes-swap parties.

February
7

Keeping Warm

There is no point in paying to heat your home if much of the warmth escapes through the roof and walls. Without insulation, up to half the heat is wasted. Stopping warmth seeping out can reduce your home's carbon emissions by up to one ton every year.

There are different options, depending on your house design. Insulating walls makes the biggest savings, but you need to do some research or talk to a professional about the options.

Up to 15 percent of your heat may be escaping through your roof, and many people tackle loft insulation themselves. If you are buying materials, insulation made from natural sheep's wool is a great product— it's hard-wearing, naturally fire-retardant and sustainable, requiring less energy to make than standard materials. Loft insulation containing recycled glass is also available.

There are also smaller jobs you can do yourself, like covering the hot water tank with an insulating jacket, lagging pipes and sealing skirting boards and using door snakes on doors. The materials are available in any hardware shop. Check whether any grants are available from your energy company, local government or charities.

February 8

Make Candles

People have been using candles for light for centuries. Unfortunately, the most common ones found today are petroleum-based, and not a good choice environmentally. Synthetic colors and fragrances can cause irritation. However, you can make your own from natural resources. Natural wax can be made from beeswax (expensive), vegetable wax or tallow.

First, gather some fireproof containers or molds. Center a wick in the middle of the container. Next, melt the wax (natural waxes can be bought at craft and nature stores). The temperature and time for melting will depend on the amount and type of wax you use. When the wax has completely melted, add any color or fragance—as with the wax, check that dyes and scents are made from all-natural sources. Allow the wax to cool slightly, then pour into the molds, checking that the wick remains centered. Allow the candles to cool overnight, then let them cure for a few days.

You can make your candles in any variety of shapes, colors, scents and sizes. Light a couple and invite someone over to enjoy an organic candlelit dinner!

February 9

Energy-Efficient Appliances

Kitchen, laundry and entertainment appliances account for a big chunk of our home's energy footprint. US home electricity use is predicted to double between 2003 and 2025 – for every greener model being developed, a bigger, more power-hungry gadget is also coming onto the market. Unless we have a renewable power source, every time we switch on an appliance, somewhere down the line carbon dioxide is released and fossil fuels are burned up.

When buying appliances, follow the tips in the panel to reduce their environmental impact—and save money!

Appliance Science

☞ *Do you really need a new one? Can you borrow it or do without? Lots of energy is needed to make and ship your new product, even if it is more efficient. An upgrade may use more power—a flat-screen TV uses three times the energy of a traditional one.*

☞ *Research before you shop: use online sites to learn how much energy is used by a host of different makes and models.*

☞ *Look for the logo: In North America, the energy star tells you the equipment is efficient. In Europe, look for A-rated goods.*

☞ *Ask in store: show store owners that their customers care about the planet.*

February 10

Palm Oil

Palm oil is cheap to grow and has been cultivated sustainably for centuries in Africa and elsewhere. But now it turns up in all manner of processed foods, in detergent, lipstick and fuels for our cars, and its mass production is having a devastating effect on natural habitats across the world.

Rainforest in Indonesia is being destroyed forever to clear the way for palm plantations. Already half of Borneo's special ecosystem is gone, threatening animals like tigers, apes and hornbill birds. And in their place is a single crop monoculture that can't support anything like the same diversity. The palm-oil industry is seen as the biggest threat to orangutans, a species that could be extinct in the wild within twelve years.

South Asia's peatlands are also under severe pressure. The soil is very fertile, but replacing them with oil palm plantations releases huge amounts of carbon and can't be reversed.

Avoid foods containing palm oil and write to the makers of your favorite products asking them to find an alternative because of the environmental damage they cause.

See March 9 for more on the biofuels debate.

February 11

Free Range

Intensive factory farming is a pretty unpleasant life for an animal. Livestock is crammed together and dosed with plenty of antibiotics, because disease spreads fast in these overcrowded conditions. Each battery chicken lives in an area just a little larger than this open book. The result is cheaper meat, but it's a high price to pay in terms of animal welfare, nutrition and the environment.

Free range is a much more sustainable farming method. Cows eat pasture and chickens can root around in the dirt and find their own food, the way nature intended. They eat less grain, which, let's face it, could be feeding humans. Much of the waste fertilizes the ground, rather than creating tons of methane and a huge disposal headache, and drugs are not used.

Research shows that free-range meat and dairy products are more nutritious. For example, eggs have one-third less cholesterol, a quarter less fat and more vitamins and minerals. Going out of your way to buy free range meat, eggs and other products helps to support farmers who are trying to make a difference.

February 12

Sociable Sharing

There are lots of great things about living alone—your own space, freedom to walk around naked and if there are dishes in the sink, you know exactly who put them there. But if you don't share your home, you won't need to be reminded that you also have no one to share the bills with.

It's the same for your home's environmental footprint—it takes just as much energy to heat the house or do many of the chores no matter how many live there.

Now, let's not rush headlong into finding roommates just yet—you could save small amounts of energy and effort by teaming up with others in the same situation. Share trips to the store, so that only one car goes. Every time you cook together, only one cooker runs, so invite friends round for food regularly.

Borrow and share appliances. Get a bunch of friends round for movie nights or just plain old lively conversation and sharing a meal together, rather than all sitting watching your own television. Not only is it sociable and much more fun to share, but you'll be trimming your home's environmental impact all the time.

February 13

Ditch the Packaging

Aren't bananas great? Nature has provided each with its own little yellow jacket. They have no need for plastic wrapping or a polystyrene tray. But that might not be the way supermarkets approach it.

Food is often over-packaged to make it look attractive or because it is transported long distances. Much ends up in landfill and even if the packaging can be recycled, energy and raw materials are required to make it in the first place.

It's hard to take a stand on this one—you can't say "I'll buy your soup, but you keep the carton." While the onus is on producers, see the panel for what you can do to navigate the packaging maze.

Pack It In

✔ *Choose shops with loose vegetables and fruit; carry reusable bags.*

✔ *Some health food shops allow you to buy by weight, filling your own containers.*

✔ *Reject overpackaged products, or leave the excess at the checkout where it is sure to be noticed.*

✔ *Choose packaging that can be easily recycled : paper, card, glass and cans.*

✔ *Avoid mixed materials, like cardboard with a plastic window, which are hard or impossible to recycle.*

February 14

Love Me, Love My Planet

Nothing says "I love you" like lavishing time, effort and creativity on your partner. Homemade gifts are much more thoughtful and personal than those tired flowers from the gas station.

If you don't feel you are particularly artistic or you don't have weeks to prepare, don't panic! There's still time to make a simple, thoughtful gift that will put you in the good books. Plus, you know they come from the heart, not the other side of the planet.

So light the candles, put on Barry White and prepare to bring back a little genuine romance with the top do-it-yourself Valentine's tips in the panel.

All Loved Up

🌸 *Make and decorate cookies in heart shapes or with loving messages.*

🌸 *Compile your loved one's favorite songs on a CD.*

🌸 *Use recycled materials to make a personalized card.*

🌸 *Decorate a picture frame and find a really great photo of you both.*

🌸 *Cook a nice meal, visit a favorite place or just spend time together doing something you both love, rather than giving material gifts.*

February 15

The Creation of Butterflies

Butterflies feature in the myths and legends of many peoples around the world, because of their beauty, fragility and magical transformation from mere caterpillars.

The Papago people of the American Southwest believed that the earth's Creator felt sad for children, because they would inevitably age and wrinkle, losing their strength and sight. So he gathered the most beautiful colors from the sunlight and sky, leaves and flowers, and put them into a magical bag. When it was opened, out flew brightly-colored butterflies, the most beautiful sight the children had seen. And these butterflies could even sing! But the birds, who had the loveliest song, though not as beautiful or colorful, were jealous and complained. So the Creator took away the butterflies' singing and made them completely silent.

Did You Know?

❀ There are more than 15,000 species of butterfly worldwide. Some butterflies migrate thousands of miles each year, and others change colors or pattern with the season and can mimic other creatures to protect against predators.

February 16

Kyoto Protocol Day

This landmark treaty on tackling climate change so far came into effect on February 16, 2005, eight years after it was signed in the city of Kyoto, Japan. More than 180 countries have signed up to a plan of action to reduce the emissions of greenhouse gases like carbon dioxide, methane and nitrous oxide, which are causing global warming.

Industrialized countries—which, after all, emit the most gases—also agreed to binding targets to reduce emissions and to help less wealthy states develop in a sustainable way. Australia ratified Kyoto in 2008, leaving the USA as the last developed country not on board—although California's Governor Schwarzenegger has committed the most populous state to similar targets.

The increase in greenhouse gases in our atmosphere and warming temperatures is no coincidence. In the last century, CO_2 levels rose by more than 25 percent. The six hottest years since records began all occurred during the last decade.

Kyoto was a start, but emissions are still increasing, and evidence of the earth warming up, and its many devastating effects, is growing. Negotiations are already under way for a new treaty and will culminate in a major summit in Copenhagen, Denmark, in December 2009.

February
17

Start Composting

This is a good time of year to start thinking about composting, or else starting a new container while last year's compost matures. It's a great way to divert food scraps from landfill, where they release global-warming methane, and transform them into free fertilizer for your garden.

It takes months for the bugs and bacteria to break down kitchen waste into rich compost, but they start to work harder as temperatures warm up.

You can compost using a simple heap, a wooden frame with bare earth below or a specially designed plastic compost container. If you don't have a garden, check if your local authority or community garden has a municipal compost scheme, or else invest in a wormery (see June 12).

Compost Essentials

✳ Feed your heap a mix of "greens" and "browns" for the best results.

Greens:

✔ Fruit and veggie scraps and peels
✔ Grass cuttings
✔ Old flowers or plants
✔ Tea bags and coffee grounds

Browns:

✔ Dead leaves
✔ Twigs, stems and branches (cut up)
✔ Cardboard (not glossy)

Be sure to leave out:

✗ Cooked food
✗ Meat and diary products
✗ Weeds with seed heads
✗ Any animal waste

Dishes to Fishes

Anyone pouring a bottle of bleach into local pond would be considered an environmental criminal.

But when laundry detergents, hair dye, mouthwash and cleaners are flushed down the sink, many of the toxic chemicals end up in the water system. Waste-water treatment isn't set up to filter out household chemicals, so many substances are simply discharged.

Scientists have found fragrance molecules in fish tissue and they know that chemicals in detergent disrupt fish reproduction. It's not just bad news for fish. Our precious water supply is part of a cycle, so rivers end up in the sea, in clouds, in rain and eventually back in the sink. We are polluting a resource upon which we rely.

It may not be on the same scale as industrial pollution of our rivers and seas, but with every household washing a cocktail of chemicals down the drain, it all adds up.

Try to cut down on chemicals in the home and use green or natural household cleaners and toiletries. Don't pour paint or other chemicals down the sink; contact your local government to ask about safe and responsible disposal.

February 19

International Whale Day

On this day in 1986, the international moratorium on commercial whaling marked a significant breakthrough in efforts to protect whales from extinction. Since then, some species that were on the brink are no longer endangered, including humpback whales and the southern right whale —an important conservation success!

Whales are among our most majestic and mysterious mammals. From the giant blue whale, at 120 tons the earth's largest creature, to the pale Artic Beluga whale, just 15 feet long, they are awe-inspiring. Whales are found in all the oceans and many migrate from tropical to polar seas during their breeding cycle. Most live in pods, and their distinctive calls are thought to help them echolocate (sonar navigation) and communicate with each other.

The international ban is under threat, though. Under its terms, some 2,000 whales can be caught each year by indigenous peoples

and for science. Now some countries are threatening to defy the ban, and Norway has already withdrawn. The impact of increased use of sonar by ships and warming seas on whale populations is also unknown. It would be a tragedy if we lost these magical creatures.

Learn more from the Whale and Dolphin Conservation Society.

Reusing Textiles

Much of reducing our eco-footprint is extending the lifespan of the things we have. And the great thing about textiles—whether they are curtains or clothes—is their flexibility. There are hundreds of ways of using them.

The trick is to reuse them at their highest level. If it's still wearable, donate it to a thrift store or charity shop. If it won't do the job any more, can the fabric be used for something else? Could you make a different garment, or a child's toy or doll clothing? Or perhaps just use it as a cleaning rag? If it's just too worn out, recycle it—it will be shredded and given a new lease of life as stuffing for furniture and car bodies.

Ways To Reuse Textiles

❀ *Use old sheets to protect carpets and furniture from messy home improvements.*

❀ *Make your own gift-bags: take two squares of cloth, sew up three sides on the inside and thread a ribbon around the top to make a drawstring close.*

❀ *Use old textiles as cleaning rags: threadbare towels make absorbent, reusable kitchen cloths*

❀ *Bring back patchwork! Start with something small like a cushion cover out of pretty fabrics.*

February 21

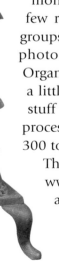

Freecycling

Offer: *Four boxes of books*
Taken: *New dining room table and chairs*
Wanted: *Pogo stick, any condition*

So reads the average freecycle mailing list. Freecycling is a global movement to keep stuff out of landfill and extend the life of the things we buy. Members join a web group covering their local area. Since it started in 2003, more than 4,500 groups have formed in 75 countries—that's a total of 6,000,000 members!

Based on the principle that one person's junk is another's treasure, members post items they want to give away or need and await responses. No money may change hands and there are a few restrictions on what can offered—some groups won't allow live animals or anything photocopied or taped for legal reasons. Organizing collections and pick-ups involves a little admin, but the upside is getting great stuff for free and helping to cut waste in the process. Freecycle organizers reckon they keep 300 tons of stuff out of landfill every day.

There are other, similar networks too. Try www.freeuse.org; www.reuseitnetwork.org; and www.sharingisgiving.org (including links to many smaller groups).

February 22

Dreaming of Summer

If thoughts are turning to vacation, and no one would blame you, spare a thought for the planet. You don't need to fly halfway across the world to get away from it all. With a little imagination, there are many adventures nearby.

One of the highlights of travel is enjoying natural environment. But travel can also threaten the planet, like aviation burning fossil fuels and releasing greenhous gases or too many tourists damaging fragile eco-systems. But we can make our trips sustainable and reduce negative impacts. See the panel for ideas.

Eco-break Ideas

❀ *Consider a car, boat, train or pedal-powered trip. If you do fly, go direct, as much of the fuel is used taking off and landing.*

❀ *Is there somewhere to vacation closer to home? Many of us never explore the beautiful areas on our doorstep. Plus, the money saved in transport costs will pay for a few swanky dinners.*

❀ *Wherever you go, look for green accommodation.*

❀ *If you do go abroad, use a responsible travel company (www.ecotourdirectory.com and similar sites have listings). Spend your money in locally owned restaurants, hotels and shops, so the community, not multinationals, profit.*

February 23

Naturally Lovely Locks

A long, long time ago, before our favorite shampoo brands were invented, people still washed their hair. Using natural goodies, the results can be just as good.

Brown sugar, for example, is great for curly hair and for reducing the build-up of other products: rub some into the scalp and rinse out after a few minutes. Give some of these treats a try, and by ditching commercial toiletries even once every week, you'll soon be cutting down on packaging and the chemicals most of them contain.

Natural Hair Treats

Baking Soda:

✔ Mix a spoonful with a little water and scrub your hair with the paste, rinse and repeat.

Cucumber Cocktail:

✔ Blend an egg, spoon of olive oil and a 3-inch piece of cucumber. Leave for 10 minutes and rinse with cool water (or the egg will scramble!) for silky hair. A beaten egg is good too.

Rinse and Shine:

✔ Rinse hair in chamomile tea to bring out blondeness or green tea for shine. Dilute beer in three parts water and pour over hair for a final rinse for extra shine. Diluted cider vinegar (two spoons in a pint of water) does the same job.

Grow Your Own

Producing your own food may seem daunting, but it's a rewarding way to get the freshest, tastiest food.

First think about space. Everyone can grow something edible, if only in window boxes, patio containers or among ornamental plants. Next, if you're growing outdoor plants, consider your climate and soil. If it's poor or doesn't drain, try making a raised bed.

If you don't already have a vegetable patch, it's not too late to plan for this season. The ideal time to dig the ground and fertilize is approaching winter, but you can catch up. Dig the soil again a month before sowing and rake it just before you plant seeds.

Include room for a compost container (not too close as it attracts bugs) and a water butt.

Lastly, plan which delicious goodies you are going to grow, and order organic seeds.

Did You Know?

❀ *Varying where each vegetable grows protects against disease and keeps the soil nutritious. If you have room, plan four beds. In the first, grow potatoes and root vegetables. In number two, brassicas. The third is for beans and peas and lastly, salad crops. Next year, rotate the positions so each crop moves up one bed.*

February 25

Fair Trade

Fair-trade Fortnight starts in the UK around this time of year. Choosing products with the fair-trade mark ensures that small-scale farmers get a decent price for their crops, but also gives a bonus for community projects that include environmental measures.

Coocafe is a co-operative of 3,500 coffee farmers in the high mountains of northern Costa Rica. With the fair-trade premium, they have funded local social and environmental improvements.

Water use in the coffee-processing plant has been slashed by 90 percent. The co-op has supported farmers to go organic and started an organic fertilizer project. Money from fair trade has also funded tree planting on an impressive 12,000 acres, an eco-tourism project and education for farmers in sustainable farming.

Across the world, a fair price for commodities makes life better for the growers and their families, as well as helping to protect the

environment. Fair-trade farmers are, by definition, small producers who understand the importance of sustainable production.

Choose fair-trade goods, particularly for crops that aren't available locally, like coffee, tea, sugar, chocolate and bananas. Check out www.fairtrade.net

February 26

Turn It Off!

The Carbon Trust estimates that businesses could cut energy use and bills by 10 percent without spending a penny. The average office has an increasing number of machines and gadgets that devour electricity.

Here are some simple ideas for saving energy and money at work, cutting carbon emissions in the process. And if you have home computer equipment, don't forget to switch it off too!

See also February 4 and October 30 to find more green office tips.

Office Ideas

❀ Turn off your computer during your lunch break, meetings and at night. You will cut its energy use by 30 percent and help it last longer. Screensavers are not energy savers, so turn off your monitor when you leave your desk.

❀ Keep lighting and heating systems well maintained to work at their most efficient. Lighting the average office overnight uses as much electricity as making 1,000 hot drinks, so turn off the lights when you leave.

❀ Make sure xerox machines and printers are switched off overnight and choose efficient equipment when you make new purchases.

February 27

Cradle to Cradle

In 2002, architect William McDonough and chemist Michael Braungart published a book they hoped would cause a revolution in our throwaway society. *Cradle-to-Cradle: Remaking the Way We Make Things* argued that a shift in the principles of design could result in a whole host of sustainable, eco-effective products.

They believe industry should be inspired by natural processes, in which the waste from one thing has a useful purpose somewhere else. Instead of a "take-make-waste" philosophy, manufacturing processes should be sustainable cycles.

Even the book was printed on a form of synthetic paper made from recycled plastic. Not only is it waterproof, but it can be dropped in the recycling when it's no longer needed.

The pair developed a cradle-to-cradle certificate for goods that have passed tough standards. They must use safe materials, incorporate materials reuse, use renewable energy and make responsible use of water. All kinds of products, from surfboard wax to office chairs, building materials to diapers, have been certified. Read more on their website: http://mbdc.com

Nature's Gifts

Until the 1970s, almost all our medications and drugs derived from nature, and the healing properties of plant extracts is still a major starting point for scientists developing new treatments.

Up to 2,000 tropical forest plants have been found to have anti-cancer properties, but our investigations are at an early stage. Because they grow in such intense and diverse ecosystems, plants have developed increasingly complex natural chemicals to help them adapt and survive within their natural environment.

But rainforest is being lost at a startling rate. We risk destroying whole species before we learn how they might be used to promote human health. The potential for cures and treatments awaiting discovery highlights just one way damaging rainforest is not in our best interests, never mind those of the natural world.

One study found a quarter of all American prescriptions derived from plants.

Some Plant-based Potions

❀ Quinine, used to treat malaria, found in cinchona tree bark.

❀ Ephedrine, a decongestant and asthma treatment, from plants in the ephedra family.

❀ Morphine, a strong painkiller found in opium poppies.

❀ Aspirin, an anti-inflammatory and blood thinner, was originally derived from willow bark.

February 29

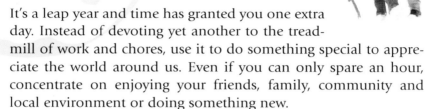

An Extra Day!

It's a leap year and time has granted you one extra day. Instead of devoting yet another to the treadmill of work and chores, use it to do something special to appreciate the world around us. Even if you can only spare an hour, concentrate on enjoying your friends, family, community and local environment or doing something new.

Wrap up warm, take a long walk with friends in a beautiful place and then come home for tea and cake. If there are spring flowers in your garden, it's a perfect time to press them for later craft use. Why not go treasure-hunting at your local salvage yard, antique store or charity shop? Or make a point of visiting your local green store or stop by an eco-café for lunch.

Leap-day Lore

❀ Adding an extra day keeps the calendar and seasons synchronized with the solar year, almost 6 hours longer than 365 days.

❀ Traditionally, women may only propose to a man on a leap day. In England, if he refuses, he must buy her a dress. In Denmark, the compensation is twelve pairs of gloves. In Greece, many consider it bad luck to marry during a leap year.

"The creation of a thousand forests is in one acorn."

—*Ralph Waldo Emerson*

Natural Spring Cleaning

Thoroughly cleaning your home at this time of year is an ancient tradition, with roots in Persian, early Orthodox and Jewish cultures.

It's possible to have a cleaner, greener home by skipping the toxic chemicals and using simple, natural cleaning techniques and products. A clean oven and fridge work more efficiently, so it's well worth the effort of scrubbing them. For best results and minimal expense, use a paste of baking soda and water.

Use baking soda in the garbage bin, too, to absorb nasty smells. A little olive oil can be used to polish metal and wooden furniture. Air your carpets, rugs, curtains and bedding outside on the line or hung over a drying rack to freshen them up. Dust surfaces with a damp cloth to catch dirt.

Diluted vinegar, baking soda or plain old soap and water make great all-purpose cleaners for surfaces and floors.

Use an old toothbrush to scrub tiles and bathroom and kitchen surfaces, and cleaning cloths that can be laundered for reuse.

And don't forget that when you are having a clear-out, there's always someone who will want your things! Give away your unwanted items, donate them to charity or freecycle rather than sending anything to landfill.

Fix Those Leaks!

Drip... drip... drip... there is little more annoying than the sound of a leaking faucet late at night. And it's bad for the planet, too. One drip per second can waste as much as 3,000 gallons of water over the course of a year.

Often leaks are caused by the tiny rubber washer becoming worn. Replacing it is not difficult—just ask a plumber or a handy friend if you don't feel confident about doing it yourself.

Check sinks and showers for leaks every so often and fix them as soon as you notice. Don't forget to keep an eye on outdoor hoses or sinks in the utility room.

While you are at it, why not think about installing water-efficient taps or spouts that fit inside your existing one but cut down on water use. Devices such as these can halve the water flow, and for most purposes you won't even notice the difference.

With water supplies under increased pressure throughout the world, anything we can do to cut waste is a step in the right direction.

As Benjamin Franklin once observed: "When the well is dry, we all know the worth of water."

March 3

Cook From Scratch

At the end of a long day, putting a ready meal in the microwave for a few minutes can seem more attractive than slicing and dicing ingredients to start cooking. But with tiny changes to our routine, healthier, cheaper and greener alternatives don't take much more effort.

Processed foods are usually much higher in salt, sugar and additives than consumers realize. One survey found that while home-baked cake needs just four basic ingredients, processed cakes may have twenty or more. These extras aren't there to enhance flavor or quality, but simply to prolong shelf-life. If you cook from scratch, you know exactly what's on your plate and where it comes from. Packaging is reduced and it's easier to buy local ingredients.

If you struggle to find time to cook, master a few quick, simple recipes like omelette, pasta and stir-fry and keep the basic ingredients well stocked. Cook up big batches or sauces at the weekend and fridge or freeze them for use during the week.

Simple Tomato Sauce

Sauté an onion and a clove of garlic for a few minutes. Add a can of tomatoes (or a cup of chopped fresh tomatoes and a little water). Simmer for at least 10 minutes. Add herbs and seasoning for a pizza base or use as a pasta sauce, with or without adding vegetables, beans or other extras.

Recycle Your Cycle

Each month, the Bike Station, a charity in Edinburgh, Scotland, diverts around three tons of old bicycles and parts from landfill sites and puts 100 refurbished bicycles back on the road. Some are sold to cover the charity's overheads, while others are given away.

We all know that paper can be pulped and glass bottles melted down, but many obscure objects can be recycled too. All over the world local volunteers collect and clean up old equipment and materials, getting them back in working order and giving them a new home. Tools and sewing machines are refitted and sent to the developing world; household goods are made into packs for families moving into permanent homes for the first time; scrap wood is reused for furniture repairs; old paper and cloth are sorted for use in children's craft projects.

It's worth checking out what community recycling projects operate in your area. Let friends know or even organize a collection of appropriate materials if you can. Check the websites for the National Recycling Coalition (US) or The Community Recycling Network (UK) for information on local initiatives.

March
5

All That Glitters Isn't Green

While diamonds may be a girl's best friend, precious stones and metals can be unfriendly to the environment in more ways than one.

Gems, gold, silver and other valuable commodities can mean great wealth for those countries and companies that control their extraction, but they have also fueled wars and harmed workers' health. Much gold is mined using cyanide or mercury: toxic chemicals harmful to the environment and people. And refining precious metals to remove impurities uses a lot of energy and chemicals. Making just one gold ring typically creates around 18 tons of waste and uses up to 5 tons of water!

When buying jewelry, choose vintage or second-hand, or why not borrow or swap with friends? If you are choosing an important piece for yourself or a gift, why not have an old piece remade into something new and beautiful?

Otherwise, find out where materials are from and ask for ethically sourced stones and metals. Synthetic precious stones, made in a lab rather than removed from the ground, may be an option.

See July 1 for an example of jewelry from recycled plastic.

A Breath of Fresh Air

With oil, gas and coal running out , creating choking pollution and their costs fluctuating wildly, attention has turned to affordable, sustainable alternatives.

Wind energy is a strong contender. Clean, safe and one of the most cost-effective forms of energy around, wind turbines have been springing up all over the place and are a key part of the energy solution. The fuel for wind power is free and plentiful in many locations. It's not going to run out anytime soon and creates no waste by-products or pollution. Of course, wind power emits no carbon, and while a little energy is needed to build and transport the turbines, they produce 80 times that amount in their lifetime.

Wind powers around 4.5 million households in the US at the time of this writing. It's good for the economy too—in Germany, for example, the renewable-energy industry has created a record number of new jobs. Some governments are also encouraging small-scale wind energy projects, all the more efficient because the power is used on nearby buildings. Find out more from the World Wind Energy Association.

March
7

Sealed with a Kiss

Making homemade envelopes is a delightful way to personalize your mail and reuse paper in the process. And it's simple!

The easiest way to make a template is to open out an old envelope, draw around it on light card and cut it out. Now use this outline on all kinds of interesting paper to make unique envelopes for your letters. You can make templates in as many shapes and sizes as you like by using different envelopes.

Almost any paper can be used for envelopes, though you want to avoid very heavy papers, which will increase postage, or very light papers, which may not protect your letters. Try pages of glossy magazines, pictures from old calendars, lacy doilies, old sheet music or wrapping paper. Seal with glue, a little sticky tape or a pretty sticker.

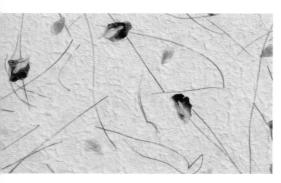

A brand new envelope isn't necessary for many items of mail. Open your own post carefully to save the best envelopes for reuse. Put a blank label over the original address and you are ready to go.

This is also a great opportunity to try out your home-made decorative stamps (January 19).

Ready, Set...GROW!

Planting from seeds rather than buying baby plants can be a more economic and satisfying way to garden. Whether you start growing them in warm conditions indoors or sow them straight in the ground depends on your local climate and crop. Follow the instructions on seed packets.

To plant inside, recycle yogurt pots and other containers to make small planters, so that soil and seed can be transplanted outside as the ground warms up. Seeds need moisture, the right temperature and air to germinate, so don't pack the soil too tightly.

Buying potting soil gives your little seedlings the best start, or try a homemade mix of good soil, compost and a little moss.

If you don't have a garden or feel unadventurous, try planting herbs in pots on your window sill (see March 19). The best time to plant for your own vegetables varies hugely. Gardeners want to get the most of the growing season, but a late frost can ruin the crop. Look up suitable times and the latest frost dates in your area on a reliable gardening site.

March 9

Biofuels

Using plants as a source of fuel is not a new idea—the very first diesel engine, invented in Germany in 1892, was designed to run on peanut oil. For many this seemed to offer a sustainable alternative to our damaging oil habit, suggesting that our current lifestyle can continue indefinitely, powered in a green, clean way. In recent years there has been a rush to grow fuel plants like corn, palm oil, wheat, soybeans and even sugar beet. A new crop can be produced each year, and the plants absorb carbon as they grow.

But the law of unintended consequences kicked in quickly. As millions of acres of farmland were converted from growing food to growing fuel, food prices soared. Valuable forest and other habitats were destroyed to make way for fuel crops, irreversibly damaging ecosystems.

All biofuels are not equal, argue green activists. Some crops provide less energy than it takes to grow them, using farm machines and petrochemical fertilizers.

Many researchers believe waste products like vegetable oil, food, wood—even sewage—can make more efficient fuels with fewer nasty side effects.

The Kakapo Bird

A flightless, nocturnal, ground-dwelling parrot—it sounds almost like a mythical creature, and there is a very real danger the Kakapo bird could become no more than that. This unique bird is the world's heaviest parrot and thrived across New Zealand before humans arrived. Earlier settlers called them "owl parrots" because of their nighttime habits and they are important in Maori myths also.

The kakapo's strong legs and claws mean it's a great climber and can reach the top of the tree canopy before parachuting down. But nesting on the ground, the population was vulnerable to new predators: cats and rats arriving with Polynesian and European settlers.

The story of the kakapo reminds us that it is so much easier to wipe a species out than bring it back from the brink. After a century of conservation work, fewer than 100 of these special birds remain, living on protected islands.

There are about 350 living species of parrot, of which 130 are considered threatened. This colorful species (right) is indigenous to Costa Rica.

March 11

Greening Your House Plants

US citizens use on average 600 L of water a day, about 150 gallons. In France, it's half that amount, but in the African state of Mali, people can access less than 3 gallons a day for washing, cooking and drinking.

Any small amount of water we can save or reuse saves valuable drinking water. Your pot plants will lap up leftover tea, the water from washing or cooking vegetables (once it has cooled), ice from the end of your drink or even old fish tank water. It's just as useful for the plants and means you don't have to pour fresh drinking water on them when they don't really need it. It's a small, but useful, water-saving habit.

While you are at it, why not think about whether any lightly used household water could be saved to use in the garden? Avoid water with chemicals or grease in it, but if you have used diluted natural cleaning products to wash floors or the car, the water can be safely used to refresh garden plants.

Community Gardens

With spring in the offing, what could be better than getting your hands in fresh earth to grow something? Getting together with others to create gardens for the whole community! In America, more than one million people are involved in community gardening schemes. And there are community-run allotments, farms, wildlife and vegetable gardens all over the world.

Most of these projects started with no more than a group of enthusiastic locals and a piece of waste ground. They provide city dwellers with a valuable haven, connecting them with the earth and where their food comes from. And often people from deprived communities and excluded groups get the chance to learn new skills and gain confidence. By doing something positive and creative, many visitors learn about their local environment and feel more inclined to protect it. Not forgetting, of course, that lots of gardens provide nutritious, locally grown fruits, salads and vegetables at minimal cost!

The National Gardening Association is a nonprofit that promotes community gardens—find out more on how to start and run one at www.garden.org or visit a project near where you live.

March 13

Beauty and the Chemical Beast

We already know that the average woman uses lots of cosmetic products each day and that there are worries about a whole range of ingredients that turn up in our bathrooms. The labels are a confusing mix of scientific and natural-sounding names, so it's hard to watch out for chemicals. The elements of perfume do not even have to be listed.

But if you are going to read the labels, here are some things you may want to watch out for:

❀ Fragrance, parfum or perfume: the most common cause of cosmetic allergies; try naturally scented or fragrance-free products.

❀ Amines and amino compounds: can form into nitrosamines during storage or in combination with other products. Nitrosamines have been found to have carcinogenic properties.

❀ Triclosan: toxic to marine animals.

❀ AHAs are used in anti-ageing creams and moisturizers. They remove a layer of skin, potentially leaving it vulnerable to sun-damage, and there are thousands of reports of adverse reactions.

❀ Parabens: a group of preservatives in toiletries that can mimic hormones with unknown consequences for human health.

See January 9 for natural homemade facemasks using fresh fruits.

Clean, Green Floors

This must be one of the hardest household chores, and dousing your floor with harsh chemicals to get the job done might seem tempting. But the greenest cleaning techniques are free of harmful chemicals and don't rely on power-hungry machines.

When you choose a new vacuum cleaner, opt for an energy-efficient one with reusable dust bags, or without bags. Alternate vacuuming with using a strong-bristled brush or manual carpet sweeper to cut power use.

For a quick carpet freshener, sprinkle baking soda, leave for 30 minutes and vacuum up.

Rugs and mats can be hung outside for airing and beaten with a tennis racket to remove dust.

Wipe hardwood floors regularly with a barely wet mop to lift the dust. Shuffle an old towel around with your feet if you need to dry the floor.

Clean tiles or stone with soap, water and a long-handled brush for extra cleaning power.

Use a doormat or adopt a no-shoes policy in your home, to cut down on the amount of dirt and debris brought inside, and save yourself extra work.

See January 20 for more natural, eco-friendly cleaning tips.

March 15

Recycling Electronics

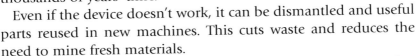

Less than half of all electronic waste is recycled at the end of its life. Dumped in landfill, toxic chemicals will seep out while bits of it will still be languishing there in thousands of years' time.

Even if the device doesn't work, it can be dismantled and useful parts reused in new machines. This cuts waste and reduces the need to mine fresh materials.

The best rule of thumb is to "reduce, reuse and recycle," in that order. Buy fewer electronic gadgets and machines—do you really need the latest designs and features? See if you can find anyone who can continue to use your device when you no longer need it.

If not, find out if your local authority accepts electronic goods for recycling. If not, ask them to start! Also try community recyclers and businesses—there's a good trade in second-hand computer parts and cell phones, for example. Or, email the manufacturer and ask where their goods can be recycled. At the very least, this influences their thinking about what their customers want.

Make sure that you erase the contents of your computer before letting it go.

See also January 7 for recycling your household appliances and January 8 for rechargeable batteries.

A Step Back in Time

Fiona Houston wondered whether her Scottish ancestors had a better life in some ways than our lives today. There was only one way to find out—turn her one-room cottage into a living history experiment for one year.

Leaving the luxuries of the 21st century behind wasn't easy, and there were times Fiona questioned why she was doing it. "But I had committed to a year," she said, "and dressing up in the clothes —as crazy as that might seem—actually was a constant reminder of what I was trying to achieve." It was a quest for a simpler life; connected to where her food and other possessions came from.

Fiona lived without electricity or running water and relied on a fire for heat and cooking. She made her own candles, beer, ink and period clothes, just as 18th-century folk did, and she grew almost all her own food, or foraged it from the wild. It was tough, but she learnt a lot about what we really need and about herself.

History Lessons

Fiona missed:
❀ Music, running water (especially hot water!), chocolate, shampoo, instant communications.

Highlights of the year:
❀ Visitors, eating well, making things and becoming physically strong.

March 17

Eco-chic Hotels

It would be pointless to live an environmentally sound life at home, only to hang up our green credentials when we arrive at our vacation destination. Vacations should be fun rather than guilt trips, and with a range of eco-accommodation, there's every reason to enjoy your visit without worrying about the planet.

There isn't a global scheme for accrediting sustainable accommodation. In North America, the Green Hotels Association is a good starting point, while www.visit21.net links green tourism schemes in various European countries. Try your library for a book of green guesthouses, and it's also worth searching online once you know your destination.

When booking accommodation, consider the impact on the environment as well as the price. Ask about recycling, local food, renewable energy and water saving. Choose a family-run or locally owned hotel, so the money stays in the community rather than

going to a big corporation. And when you get there, use towels for a few days, skip the mini-shampoos, save water and turn off lights and appliances when they aren't in use, just as you would at home!

Easter Traditions

Long before Easter became an important Christian festival, folk traditions marked the changing of seasons after a long, cold winter at this time of year.

Eggs, rabbits and lambs all signify new life. Ancient Saxons ate spiced buns with a cross to honor the goddess Eostre (and Easter probably derives from that name).

To celebrate these traditions, dye hard-boiled eggs (free-range of course!) with the natural products listed in this panel, in half a cup of water and a teaspoon of vinegar. Or experiment with other colorful foods. Use rubber bands, tape and cloth to cover part of their surface for spegg-tacular results!

Why not make a recycled Easter basket to put them in? Use a cardboard box or food container, add a cardboard handle and decorate with ribbon, colorful scrap paper, lace or buttons.

Rainbow Eggs

* Yellow: *turmeric powder*
* Blue: *red cabbage*
* Red/orange: *onion leaves (you need a cup: store your cooking scraps beforehand)*
* Brown: *coffee grounds*
* Purple: *fresh beetroot*

March 19

Window-box Herbs

With your own window ledge herb garden, it's fantastic to be able to snip off a few leaves and tuck into them seconds later. You don't need acres of space or special talents or equipment to enjoy the taste all year round.

Almost any kind of container will do the job, as long as there's a hole in the bottom to prevent waterlogging. Herbs can be grown from seeds or cuttings or you can buy a plant already growing.

Try some of these panel suggestions in your cooking—usually it's best to add them at the end so the flavor remains intact.

You can also grow small salad plants in pots quite easily—try arugula (rocket), lettuces, cherry tomatoes and chili peppers.

Chef's Herb Garden

❀ *Parsley: its refreshing bite is good with potatoes, rice and casseroles.*

❀ *Mint: grows profusely, delicious with summer fruit, and makes a great tea.*

❀ *Basil: one herb that's definitely best fresh! Use whole leaves in Italian dishes and salads.*

❀ *Chives: snip with scissors and serve in salads or as a classy soup garnish*

❀ *Coriander: try adding flavorsome stalks and chopped leaves to your curries, chili, guacamole and hummus.*

It's Good to Share

There are a whole host of things that are incredibly useful for jobs that come along only once in a while, but spend the rest of the time taking up space and gathering dust. Rather than having a cupboard or shed full of every kind of equipment, you could downsize by sharing with neighbors and friends. It sociable, space-saving, thrifty and cuts down on the raw materials and energy needed to make one each.

You may want to set up a formal arrangement with like-minded neighbors, whereby a group lists useful items for sharing. Or maybe you simply want to start asking around those you know before purchasing a new tool or piece of equipment.

Some suggestions are listed in the panel of things we don't need to own ourselves, but might want to use periodically.

Share Alike

❀ *Tools, from basics like a plunger and hammer to power-tools.*
❀ *Paint brushes, wallpaper stripper and other decorating equipment.*
❀ *A step-ladder*
❀ *Gardening tools and lawnmower*
❀ *Picnic hamper*
❀ *Large suitcases*
❀ *Ice cream maker, juicer and other kitchen gadgets just for special recipes or occasions*

March 21

World Forestry Day

The autumn equinox in the southern hemisphere was chosen for World Forestry Day, to celebrate the contribution of forests to the community.

For millennia, humans have used forests and their products to meet our basic needs of shelter, food and fuel, with their natural beauty providing inspiration for generations. Now we know, too, that trees have a vital role in absorbing the carbon dioxide we produce by burning fossil fuels, slowing climate change.

Half of all the world's original forest cover is already gone, and only one-fifth is untouched by human life. Across the world, rainforest, alpine woods and ancient deciduous forests are under threat from logging, agriculture, industry, roads, pollution and changing weather. When the trees go, the fragile ecosystem can't

survive intact: animals, insects and smaller plants are disrupted or eliminated altogether, and soil can be washed away.

Americans use a quarter of the wood commercially harvested worldwide—the equivalent of one ancient tree per person per year. Other Western lifestyles can be equally destructive. One small step we can all take on World Forestry Day is to resolve to use only recycled or sustainable wood and paper products.

The Power of the Oceans

Flowing water has long been used to generate power, but only now are engineers developing machines that can harness the power of the waves.

Let's face it—there's no shortage of ocean power. And with a dependable ebb and flow of the tide twice each day, it's a good resource for coastal areas. Wind also whips up waves that crash onto the shore. Capturing and turning that power into electricity could be key to meeting our ongoing energy needs.

The World Energy Council calculated that the oceans could generate twice the amount of electricity the world currently uses.

Wave and tidal power are in their infancy. The world's first commercial wave power farm opened in 2008, off the Portuguese coast. Researchers are experimenting with turbines on the seabed that turn with the tides, and pontoons that float on top, as well as investigating how best to convert it to usable electricity.

There have been worries about how devices may impact on sea life and the shoreline, but with time and experience these issues will be resolved. Find out more by checking online for the latest developments in this fast-growing area.

Foraging for Seaweed

Seaweed is one of nature's best free gifts. It has been used as a food, a medicine, a beauty product, a fertilizer and even a roofing material (in coastal areas of Denmark). And then there are the magical names—Sea Lettuce, Irish Moss, Bladderwrack and Sugarkelp among them.

Check with local nature groups for what species are common on your beach—not all seaweeds are edible (though they are rarely harmful). Spring low tides are the best time for collecting, below the tide line. Only take small amounts and cut the strands, leaving the anchorlike "holdfast" attached so the plant can regrow.

Many different varieties can be dried or eaten fresh. Carrageen, or Irish Moss, makes fine puddings. Dulce can be dried for a chewy snack. A handful of kelp, boiled up with mushrooms and vegetables, makes an excellent soup.

See September 10 for more foraging tips.

Skin Conditioner

❀ *Try something different: On Ireland's west coast, a seaweed bath is a luxurious beauty treatment. Rinse half a bucket of wrack-type seaweed, before putting it in a hot bath. It releases oils and minerals leaving skin and hair deliciously soft and silky.*

Carrot ♥ Leek

Plants and insects interact with each other in the wild, and smart gardeners use their knowledge of how. By using the likes and dislikes of different creatures, you can keep pests off your crops and attract friendly creatures.

This is companion planting, a wonderful way to harness the natural qualities of plants for a more productive garden. Simply by planting neighboring crops that mask attractive scents or act as a decoy, you can prevent hungry bugs from getting a foothold. Deterring pests in the first place reduces the temptation to resort to harmful chemical pesticides.

Plant carrots and leeks next to each other—the smell of carrots repels leek moth, while leeks' odor scares off carrot fly.

French marigolds, chives or basil next to your tomatoes will ward off aphids, greenfly and blackfly. Marigolds also attract caterpillars away from cabbages, and they deter eelworm, which is harmful to growing potatoes.

Grow garlic among your roses for beautiful, aphid-free flowers.

The herbs dill and yarrow attract a number of "good" insects to your garden beds, like hoverflies and ladybugs, which eat other garden pests.

The Green Man

A solemn face peering out from dense leaves, the Green Man reminds us of our union with nature and the rebirth of all that is green and lush as winter gives way to spring and the annual cycle of new life and growth begins again.

His enigmatic mask stares down from pillars and walls in European churches, Indian temples, in Malaysia, Borneo and Nepal as well as in poems, songs and old stories. He's even been seen on the walls of banks in New York and Chicago.

The leaf-mask figure's origins are an ancient mystery, though he turns up where there are old woodlands. There are theories that he represents the Spirit of the Woods, the spirit of life and the power of rebirth, particularly at this time of the year.

In the town of Clun in rural England, the Green Man Festival is celebrated on the first day of May. He does battle with the spirit of winter on the town's bridge, and his victory is celebrated with a three-day festival and the crowning of a May queen. Shown at left is the Green Man at York Minster, northern England

Good to the Last Drop

It can seem a lot of labor to get every last bit of peanut butter out of the jar and onto your sandwich, but taking the time to scrape means less waste. If it becomes our habit to get one more portion out of every pot, carton, tube and bottle, it will all add up. Here are some hints to help:

Ensure that you have a good bowl scraper to get the last bits when you are baking. Use it also to get the tricky bits out of jars.

Use the paper that your butter was wrapped in to grease baking trays, so that you use the very last traces.

When you use canned tomatoes or sauces, put a little water in the empty container, swirl it around to get the last remnants, and add it to the contents of your pan.

Leave bottles of cosmetics and dish-washing liquid upside down when nearly empty so that it's easier to get every last drop.

Cut open a tube of toothpaste when it's impossible to squeeze any more out. Persevere, and you will find there's enough left in the tube for at least three or four more brushes.

March 31

Dip a Toe in the Water

Even small water features will attract frogs, toads and newts to your garden, and they can be valuable snail and insect eaters, protecting your vegetables. In many places, amphibians are in serious decline and these watery oases will be a lifeline.

Site your water feature in the sun and ensure gently sloping sides to attract maximum wildlife and minimize danger.

Many people create one simply by digging a hole and lining it with thick plastic sheeting. Put in a layer of soil, to allow water-dwelling plants to grow. Avoid keeping fish in your pond if you want frogs to breed, as they consider frogspawn a tasty treat.

If you don't have room for a pond, consider sinking a barrel, old sink or large bucket to make a mini one. This will still attract insects and amphibians, adding to the natural diversity.

Ponds need a little maintenance to remain at their best. If too much algae builds up, remove it with a stick or net—your pond may need more plants which act as natural filters. The National Wildlife Federation has useful factsheets on its website.

I wander'd lonely as a cloud
That floats on high o'er vales and hills,
When all at once I saw a crowd,
A host, of golden daffodils;
Beside the lake, beneath the trees,
Fluttering and dancing in the breeze.

Continuous as the stars that shine
And twinkle on the Milky Way,
They stretch'd in never-ending line
Along the margin of a bay:
Ten thousand saw I at a glance,
Tossing their heads in sprightly dance.

The waves beside them danced; but they
Out-did the sparkling waves in glee:
A poet could not but be gay,
In such a jocund company:
I gazed—and gazed—but little thought
What wealth the show to me had brought:

For oft, when on my couch I lie
In vacant or in pensive mood,
They flash upon that inward eye
Which is the bliss of solitude;
And then my heart with pleasure fills,
And dances with the daffodils.

—William Wordsworth

April
1

Kona Earth Festival

For many visitors, Hawai'i is paradise on earth. And residents know how sensitive and fragile their beautiful environment is. Around 90 percent of Hawaiian flowers, including the beautiful hibiscus kokio, are not found anywhere else in the world, and the fertile volcanic soils and delicate coral reefs offer a very special ecosystem.

In 2006 the community of Kona on the Big Island's coast decided that the environment was so important to them that Earth Day (22 April) should be upgraded to a whole month of practical action, celebrations and awareness-raising for the planet.

From recycled art and fashion shows, to film screenings, an organic farm and food tour and, of course, a "surf for the earth" event, the grassroots festival has captured the imagination of a host of local groups and businesses. And to leave a lasting legacy for the environment, there are also projects to plant native trees and improve local paths and trails.

Is there anything similar in your neighborhood? For more inspiration visit their website: www.konaearthfestival.org.

Make Use of April Showers

It seems a little crazy to pour drinking-quality water on the garden, on the car or down the toilet. Using rainwater where appropriate cuts the expense and energy needed to treat and transport water.

Install a rain barrel/water butt—a large container that collects water that falls on your roof direct from the drainpipes. Even a large butt can fill in less than an hour in a heavy downpour. When you need to water the garden or clean the car, a tap at the base of the barrel allows you to fill a bucket or watering can.

Very keen greens should check out systems for using rainwater indoors as well. The practice goes back to pre-Roman times, but now makes use of modern technology to harvest rainwater, store it underground and divert it to the washing machine and toilet cistern. It can halve your household's drinking-quality water use.

If your area has dry summers or water shortages all year round, collecting and storing runoff is crucial. Start now by placing a bucket outside when a heavy shower threatens. This rainwater butt (right) is at CERES Community Environment Park, Melbourne, Australia.

Find out more at the Rainwater Harvesting Association.

April
3

Greener Schools

Cutting energy and water use in school buildings can make a huge difference, given their size and number. But it's also crucial for young people to see green improvements in action, not just learn about them in theory.

Parents, teachers and members of the local community can all help schools to be greener. Here are some good starting points:

❀ Start a school garden to attract wildlife and grow vegetables. Include a compost heap.

❀ Involve the whole school in collecting drink cans. Aluminum is valuable and recycling companies will buy large quantities. A trip to see new cans made from old would be an excellent field trip.

❀ The average school spends more on energy than books–switch computers off when not in use, turn out lights and consider a solar panel or wind turbine.

❀ More and more children are driven to school. A "walking bus" safely escorts pupils on foot. Also encourage parents to carpool.

❀ A plan to cut water use through efficiency and education can halve a school's water bills.

❀ Find more information and plenty of fresh ideas on Eco-School International's website.

Go Direct to the Source

Farmers' markets have exploded in popularity. Wherever they are, the basic principles remain the same: farmers and producers selling directly to consumers, and all within a small radius. As well as the freshest vegetables and fruit, locally reared meat and cheese, many sell farm-made jams, bread and tasty home-baking. You might also find other green businesses and local artisans selling their crafts.

Shopping at your local farmers' market allows you to build a relationship directly with the farmer. It cuts out the middleman, and his hefty slice of the profit, so those who grow the food get a better price. It's about the preservation of small-scale farming, and also building community and making responsible green choices based on face-to-face knowledge about where food comes from.

If you don't have a farmers' market nearby, ask local farmers where you can buy their produce. Many sell direct to the public. Look out for signs on farm gates or contact organizations like the North American Farmers' Direct Marketing Association (it also has international members) for local suppliers.

April
5

Moth Matters

Moths have a poor reputation compared with their beautiful butterfly cousins. Often they're seen as pests or considered plain and drab. These remarkable creatures have their benefits, though. They are a vital part of our wildlife food chain, feeding birds, bats and mammals. Some, like the humming-bird hawkmoth, pollinate flowers and plants. The larvae of other species even produce silk.

Moths can be found in all kinds of habitats, often cleverly mimicking trees or plants. Others have bright markings and are as colorful as any butterfly. Most species are nocturnal, though some are up and about during the day.

As for their pest qualities, very few species like to nibble on clothes. If you do need to deter them from your wardrobe, the scent of lavender or cedar wood should do the trick, or if clothing is infested, freeze it for a few days.

Moths and their caterpillar larvae can cause major damage to crops and plants. One way to limit the damage is to attract natural predators, another reason to avoid spraying chemicals. In your vegetable patch, watch for caterpillars and pull them off affected plants by hand.

Recycling in the Garden

Everywhere in the garden, it's clear that natural cycles are anything but wasteful. One system's byproduct can be useful somewhere else—dead leaves, for example, become prime quality mulch, protecting plants during the cold winter months. Nature's way of using things again is something we want to copy as we try to use and waste less.

Composting leftover food is a great example of recycling for the benefit of your garden, but there are lots more things we can do.

Large plastic drink bottles make excellent "cloches," small domes that keep individual plants warm and frost-free in the early spring. Cut in two and place each half over a seedling.

If you have problems with birds landing on your vegetables or eating the seed, tie some old or scratched CDs on a string across the patch, or use the tape from damaged video cassettes.

Use cardboard egg cartons or yogurt pots to plant seeds indoors. Once they grow and the risk of frost is past, replant outside.

Creative folk may like to experiment with garden decorations, birdbaths, yardbirds or sculptures made from all kinds of found objects.

April 7

World Health Day

It's easier for a healthy planet to support healthy people. There is significant evidence that climate change will become an increasingly serious barrier to improving the life of the world's poorest people.

With extreme pressure on water sources, rising temperatures and falling agricultural yields, poor families will find it harder to get safe, clean drinking water, sanitation and enough food to be strong and healthy. Climate change is predicted to critically reduce water during the dry season for a sixth of the world's population.

A lack of water and sanitation facilities poses health and environmental challenges. When water supplies are contaminated, disease spreads like wildfire. Without proper systems to dispose of human waste, it is dumped untreated on land or in rivers. Over time, water and soil quality are damaged.

But improved sanitation protects people, their livelihoods and their environment. The charity Water Aid has estimated that for every dollar spent on sanitation and education, up to $9 is saved in healthcare costs and lost productivity. Thinking about the global situation highlights why tackling climate change and saving water is so urgent.

The Benefits of Walking

It may not be the fastest way to get about, but it is carbon-free, keeps you trim, fit and healthy and is just the right pace to explore your neighborhood or a new city.

Walking at a moderate pace burns up to 300 calories an hour and has been shown to reduce the likelihood of heart disease, high blood pressure, osteoporosis, depression and stress. Whether you're hiking up a mountain, strolling in the park or simply getting from A to B, walking is a low-impact sport for your body, your wallet and the environment.

For those who want to be green, though, it's not just a form of exercise, but a form of transport. Leaving the car at home and walking instead of using public transport where possible cuts down fossil-fuel use and carbon emissions.

Try to build it into your everyday schedule, whether you walk to work, school, shopping or meeting friends for a stroll. Plan the journeys you can make on foot from your home. If your town lacks trails and sidewalks, contact your local authority to ask for improvements.

April 9

Baking Up Birthday Treats

What present do you get for the person who has everything? So many of us have more knick-knacks than we know what to do with. And whose heart has not sunk at unwrapping a singing fish or similarly tacky gift?

Enough is enough! Let's make birthdays and special occasions about delicious treats, not more clutter. Baked with love, who wouldn't prefer a gift of homemade cake, cookies or muffins?

Choose the best, organic ingredients and select a recipe to your friend's tastes. Consider decorations too, whether you are making magical cupcakes with icing and sprinkles or a giant cake with an appropriate message. Why not try a themed cake that reflects their interests—maybe a hobby, their job or a favorite place or activity; the options are limited only by your creativity!

A batch of your best cookies or muffins in an attractive box or basket makes a thoughtful gift. Most people will value the time and energy you put into it, much more than an unnecessary ornament or gadget. And after all, it's virtually impossible to have too much cake!

Perpetual Produce

There are some amazing plants that allow you to harvest a few leaves at a time and then keep growing and replenishing the supplies. If you are careful not to overpick, one plant lasts months!

Produce that is available in cut-and-come-again varieties include many lettuces, spinach, arugula (rocket), chard and mizuna—all the ingredients you need for a tasty, fresh and absolutely local salad!

They are mostly easy to grow in the garden, squeezed in between other veggies, or in pots or window boxes, as they don't need very deep soil. Some kinds are even hardy enough for fall and winter— cover with a homemade cloche (see April 6), newspaper or a gardener's fleece should temperatures dip toward freezing.

Plant seeds in a sunny spot, in composted earth, several per pot or in rows a foot apart. Keep the soil moist.

Start taking leaves once the plant is 2 inches tall and pick regularly to encourage plenty of growth. By this method, you can have a variety of fresh salad leaves just when you want to eat them.

April 11

How Water Was Discovered

Long ago, an ancient Aboriginal story goes, Australia had no water, and the animals were thirsty. One day a little bandicoot noticed the blue-tongued lizard drying himself behind a rock. All the animals were angry and accused the lizard of hiding a secret water source.

They decided the bandicoot should follow him. But the lizard was too clever; he could see out of the corner of his eye. Then a little wagtail was chosen, because he could hide quickly. But his black-and-white tail bobbed about and gave him away. They were no closer to finding the water source. Then the rat volunteered to follow the lizard. The animals laughed and said he was too small.

The rat was hurt, but decided to try anyway. When the wily lizard thought he was being followed, the tiny rat jumped out of

the way. He led the rat right to a spring under a flat rock. The animals were delighted; they praised the rat and played in the water. The kingfisher made creeks with his beak, all the way down to the sea.

So don't feel disheartened if you are think you are too small to make a difference. You'll be amazed what you can do!

Natural Scrub

All it takes is a few seeds, nurtured into a large green vegetable, and a little aftercare to produce your very own, home-grown shower loofah—the ultimate local, green product.

A near relative of the zucchini plant, seeds to grow your own loofah are widely available in seed catalogues.

The plant needs quite a long, frost-free growing season, so plant it out when the last frost is over, or start them inside. Best grown on a trellis or fence, you can also eat the produce when small. But for the lovely, exfoliating sponges, wait until the first frost to harvest, when they are larger.

To transform your beautiful vegetable into a bathtime treat, peel the outer skin and squeeze under the tap to wash out the seeds and fleshy part and leave to dry. The fibrous shell should by now begin to resemble a shower loofah.

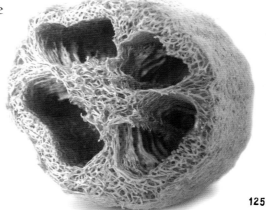

Save a few of the seeds and you are ready to plant out next year's crop of home-grown sponges and plant a few extra for unusual gifts.

April
13

Asparagus

At this time of year, asparagus is one of the first vegetables to poke its head above ground and yield edible stuff. And what a tasty sign of things to come! It's got a reputation as a luxury crop. Tuck into a plate just picked and sautéed with butter—it's not hard to see why.

Asparagus is a truly remarkable plant. Spears rise rapidly from the garden in early spring and are at their best harvested and eaten that very day. Once it's picked, the sugars in the plant start to turn to starch. Well-traveled, refrigerated or tinned, an asparagus spear is a pale shadow of its former self.

Growing asparagus is a long-term commitment. For the first three years, you must resist the temptation to pick any, allowing the plant to become established. After that, expect eight weeks of fresh stalks for many years to come. Asparagus likes deep, well-drained soil and lots of compost, manure or seaweed in autumn.

It's only worth buying asparagus from local sources —try your farmers' market. In North America, asparagus can be found growing wild if you know where to look.

Polar Bears in Peril

Topping the Artic food chain, polar bears can weigh up to 1,700 pounds and be as much as 10 feet tall. They are specially adapted for life in one of earth's harshest habitats with a double layer of fur and a big appetite for seal, walrus and even small whales.

Scientists believe that there are around 22,000 bears roaming near the North Pole, in northern Russia, Alaska, Canada, Greenland and Svalbard, Norway. In winter, they cross the sea ice to hunt. In summer months, bears live off body fat reserves and some come onto land as the ice retreats.

And ice is melting earlier and faster than ever before. As the summer stretches and the ice retreats, polar bears are in trouble. Reaching the sea ice to feed is only possible later in the year, and the winter feeding season is shorter. In some places, populations are in decline and the average weight of bears is falling.

In 2004, four bears drowned trying to swim back to pack ice off the Alaskan shore. The prospect of further climate change is the biggest threat to the survival of these magnificent beasts. Find out more and updated information at the Polar Bears International website.

April 15

Recycling CDs

If you no longer listen to the same tunes as your teenage self, clearing out the old records and CDs remains both an emotional wrench and a recycling challenge.

The best solution for undamaged goods is to pass them on to someone else who will enjoy listening to them. The usual methods—thrift shop, yard sale, freecycle and online sites—apply here. You could also try swapacd.com and titletrader.com, which are websites specializing in swapping music and movies.

If they are scratched, the materials can be recycled. CDs, DVDs and their cases can be refurbished to be used again or made into insulating material, burglar alarms and bicycle reflectors. The tricky thing is finding a specialist company that does the recycling. There may be a charge for disposal and postage, though you may consider getting those embarrassing '80s albums safely (and greenly) out of the way is a price worth paying. Alternatively, consider using them around the home or in crafts. Old CD cases will store jewelry neatly, while a bunch of CDs could be framed or turned into coasters or a mobile.

Downshifting

If you're stressed, busy and feeling worn out, then International Downshifting Week is coming to your rescue around now. Downshifting means changing down a gear in life. There's no point in working so hard to pay for a lifestyle that we have no time to enjoy. It's not about opting out of the mainstream completely, but slowing down and finding satisfaction in a simpler, greener life right where you are.

Try out some of the tips for downshifting in the panel.

Gearing Down

- *Think about how you spend your time, and how you want to spend it. How can you make them a closer match?*

- *Leave work on time this week and book a half day off to spend with someone you love and haven't seen for a while.*

- *Relax and enjoy quality time with your family, rather than rushing around. Cook up a meal together, turn the TV off and play games or just talk and laugh together.*

- *Next time you have an urge for some retail therapy, try simpler, cheaper pleasures like growing or making something—remember the more money you spend, the longer you need to work to pay for it.*

April 17

WWOOF-ing

Not the racket made by noisy dogs, but World Wide Opportunities on Organic Farms. If you are a city-dweller who longs for the countryside, want to learn more about gardening and farming or simply want something a bit different for a vacation or short break, then WWOOF-ing is for you.

The scheme swaps firsthand experience on farms, smallholdings and organic gardens with extra help for the owners. You volunteer your time and labor and in return, hosts provide free accommodation, meals and plenty of inspiration. You will learn so much in a few short days, while offering practical help to organic producers, many of whom are running small family farms.

There are WWOOF-ing groups all over the world, so the opportunities are endless. By joining a national WWOOF association, for a small administration fee, you get a list of hosts to contact and

arrange your stay. The only other cost is travel.

Opportunities vary in length and type of work, from looking after cattle to growing vegetables, making hay to making jam. Children are welcomed by many hosts. Visit the WWOOF website to find out more.

World Heritage Day

Too often businesses are eager to flatten old buildings rather than restore or renovate them. It's done in the name of progress, sometimes even the environment, as new plans may include cutting-edge green features.

But modernizing our built heritage can be cheaper and use fewer raw materials than starting from scratch.

The same is true of our homes. We may long to live in a state-of-the-art eco-village, but for the majority of us, our existing dwellings will have to be adapted to support a greener lifestyle. "Retro-fitting" is where new technologies are fitted to old homes —with a little ingenuity, a traditional house can be transformed into a green paradise.

World Heritage Day has traditionally been about preserving old monuments and sites. We might think of it as valuing and working with what we've got rather than starting from scratch every time. This applies to buildings but also to green improvements in our homes. Can we adapt what's currently there rather than throwing it all out and starting again?

April 19

Choosing Furniture

Even well-known chains have been exposed for selling products made from illegally logged wood. Unregulated logging threatens the future of forests and their whole ecosystem. Always choose native rather than exotic tropical woods and opt for certified sustainable wood that displays the Forest Stewardship Council (FSC) logo.

The first question to ask when considering new furniture is: do we really need it? Can the old item be mended or freshened up with a coat of varnish or new covers? If not, can we source a replacement second-hand? Much recycled furniture is good quality, discarded when people move or redecorate rather than because it's broken or worn out.

Some furniture makers use reclaimed wood to make new pieces. A handmade item may be more expensive than a something from a furniture super-store, but you can influence the design and materials used, plus you are supporting local artisans.

When you have furniture to get rid of, try and find a good home for it. A young couple setting up home may find a well-worn old sofa is just the thing they need.

April 20

Coral Reefs

The tropical rainforests of the sea, coral reefs teem with life: fish, crustaceans, algae and sponges living in harmony with hard and soft corals. These complex ecosystems have been on the planet for 400 million years, but they are also incredibly fragile. Corals are very sensitive, needing clean, clear water to thrive. There's evidence the rate of growth is slowing in some reefs as water quality deteriorates.

The Great Barrier Reef off Australia's northeastern coast actually consists of more than 2,800 reefs. Barrier reefs like these help protect coastal areas from storm surges by absorbing wave impact.

The reef itself is formed when the skeletons of living coral organisms harden or calcify. Algae live in the outer tissues of coral, protected and supplying the coral with food. When the coral becomes stressed, these algae are expelled, causing them to lose their color and become bleached. Changes in sea temperature, even by just a degree or two, pollution or changing saltiness can cause irreversible bleaching. Along with the impact of fishing and further climate change, half of all coral reefs could be gone by 2030.

April 21

Paper Use in the Office

The average office worker gets through around 10,000 sheets of paper each year. Reducing that will save your firm money, not only in supplies, but also in printing costs, storage and disposal.

Those eight boxes of paper sitting in the stationary cupboard used to be 1.5 acres of trees, out there absorbing greenhouse gases. By using paper with a high recycled content, fewer virgin trees are cut down. Follow the guidelines in the panel, and find more from www.reduce.org.

Paper Cuts

- Add a "think before you print" message to your email signature.

- Encourage co-workers to print and photocopy on both sides of every page they use—halving the amount of paper consumed.

- Make a pad for brainstorming or notes using scrap paper blank on one side, fastened with a clip.

- Ensure there are plenty of paper recycling bins in strategic places.

- Remind the boss that cutting paper use saves money too.

- Bring in a mug rather than use paper cups for beverages (it will hold more coffee as well!)

- Switch from paper towels in the bathroom.

Earth Day

Sometimes it's not easy being green, and it can feel like you're the only one trying to make a difference. But not on Earth Day! On April 22 each year, up to a billion people take part in the biggest secular holiday in the world.

The 40th anniversary occurs in 2010 of the first annual Earth Day, founded to highlight the importance of environmental issues. Since then, green concerns have become much more prominent and mainstream, but also more urgent. The proportion of the population aware of, and acting on, local and international problems is swelling to a critical mass.

There's plenty to worry about the future of our planet, but why not do something positive to mark Earth Day? Attend a local event or organize your own—an eco-film night, organic wine and food tasting, exhibition, clean-up day or tree-planting event.

This special day isn't meant to replace our year-round efforts to tackle environmental problems, but it is a good opportunity to join millions of other concerned citizens all over the globe. To find out what's happening near you or to register your event, visit the website at www.earthday.net.

April 23

Buy Local

It's a no-brainer that locally grown food has spent less time in transit and storage, where flavor and nutrition start to fade. Long journeys also mean varieties of fruit and vegetable are picked for their suitability to travel well—not because they taste good!

Our tastes are increasingly exotic: French cheeses, New Zealand lamb and Ethiopian coffee. But we can overlook excellent local delicacies, which support the local economy and take a fraction of the energy to reach you.

Buying air-freighted food can make the CO_2 emissions from your shopping cart exceed that of your car and home combined.

Transport produce from garden to kitchen and we're talking food feet, not food miles. Buying from local farmers is next best, and most farmers' markets specify that food must be grown within a 30- or 50-mile radius. In the supermarket, select local produce and vary your shopping list to what's available. Remember the

ingredients in processed foods are likely to have clocked up thousands of miles from farm to factory before they even start the trip to the store. If you do buy long-distance groceries, choose lighter dried foods in packages like spices, sun-dried tomatoes and tea.

A Little Ray of Sunshine

Turning the rays of sun landing on your roof into energy is one of the most effective ways of generating your own renewable energy. Solar power can be used to heat hot water or to convert heat into electricity.

Even in the UK—not known as the sunniest nation—90,000 solar water heaters have been installed already. Heating water takes a lot of electricity, but these systems plug your household's plumbing into the sun's heat for carbon-free hot water. Solar energy can provide half of your water-heating needs even in overcast weather.

The alternative is photovoltaic cells. They transform the sun's heat into electricity, meeting up to half of your home's electricity requirements. Around 30 tons of carbon emissions are saved over the lifetime of one of these systems.

Both solar power units work best on a south-facing wall or roof. They are not cheap to install, though grants are sometimes available.

Or you could try it yourself! Make your own solar water heater from an old window, domestic radiator painted black, a plywood box to mount it in and some piping and plumbing bits to connect it to your water system. There's plenty of advice online.

April 25

International Penguin Day

Around this time, millions of penguins head to the same breeding sites they were born in for the southern hemisphere's winter. These birds are sociable, resilient and classy—where else would we get the penguin suit?

The 17 species include Emperor, Rockhopper, Macaroni and Fairy penguins. They are specially adapted for life at sea, and though they can't fly, penguins are excellent swimmers, divers and jumpers. When need arises, they waddle or toboggan on their fronts for many miles. In a further display of nature's genius, penguins are disguised in the ocean by their dark backs from above and their white front from below.

After elaborate mating dances, male emperor penguins hold an egg on their feet to keep it warm while the female travels miles

from these hatcheries to feed at sea. Penguins fast for long periods while they keep eggs or chicks warm or when their new coat of feathers is growing.

All species of penguins are protected by international treaties. Overall there are millions of breeding pairs, though Humboldt and African penguins are considered at risk of extinction.

The Chernobyl Explosion

In the early hours of April 26, 1986, a steam explosion occurred in Reactor 4 of Chernobyl nuclear power station. A subsequent fire spread a radioactive cloud over the Soviet Union, Europe and America's eastern seaboard.

News of the accident reached the outside world on April 27, when alarms at a Swedish nuclear power station 700 miles away detected dangerous levels of radiation. Two workers died in the initial explosion, and the UN estimates that the disaster caused 4,000 extra cases of childhood cancers. The nearby city of Pripyat remains a ghost town to this day. As well as falling in rain, highly radioactive particles were carried by the Pripyat river into rivers and lakes further afield. These materials accumulate in the food chain, and there were concerns about fish contamination as far away as Britain and Germany.

Chernobyl (memorial statue, right) is by no means the world's only serious nuclear accident. Even when nuclear power stations run safely, the question of safe disposal of spent nuclear fuel has yet to be answered: the long-term effects of storage are unknown.

Make Your Own Yogurt

Dairy products are readily available, so why make your own? Because it's fun, not nearly as hard as it sounds, and you can ensure there are no unwanted additives.

Yogurt is milk soured by particular bacteria—it sounds gross, but these ones are healthy for your digestive system. The simplest way to get hold of them is to use a little commercially bought live yogurt, though you can also buy the cultures dried.

Make sure all your equipment is very clean to start with. Put two pints of milk in a pan and heat very slowly until a skin forms. Then allow it to cool to body temperature (around 100°F/37.8°C, if you're using a thermometer).

Add two tablespoons of yogurt and fruit, fruit puree, honey or nuts if you want to add texture and flavors. Pour into jars. Keep at the same temperature and still for a few hours—wrapped in a towel inside a picnic cooler or in a pot of warm water. When it goes thick and creamy, put the jars in the fridge. To start your next batch, use two spoons of your homemade yogurt, or freeze if you aren't going to make another batch for a few days.

Greener Building Materials

Whether you are constructing a dream home from scratch or considering renovations to an existing dwelling, building work can cause a great deal of disruption, dirt and waste. A sustainable building plan aims to cut waste, make efficient use of resources and produce a building that will have minimal impact on the environment over its whole life.

Energy- and water-saving features are often easier to include in your home at the construction stage. Start by hiring an architect or builder who understands what's important to you.

Some building materials—cement, plaster, plastics and metals—are made in energy-intensive processes. Sheep's wool insulation, local slate, stone and sustainable wood use less energy in production and transportation. Avoid wood preservatives and paints that contain toxic chemicals.

Try sourcing materials from reclamation and salvage yards: beautiful doors, fireplaces and wooden floor boards may be among your finds.

Around a sixth of the wood brought to a construction site does not get used and ends up in landfill as offcuts instead. Ensure that as much leftover material is recycled or reused as possible.

April 29

Green Weddings

Your big day doesn't need to be a big drain on the earth's resources. The first trick is to prioritize simple style. From recycled paper invitations to biodegradable confetti, there are lots of things you can do to green up your wedding.

A few ideas are listed here:

❋ **Venue**: choose one that's accessible by public transport. Think outside the box—what about a community center, school or field for a luxury picnic? Make the decorations or choose local, seasonal flowers or pot plants that guests can take away.

❋ **Transport**: Encourage guests to share lifts. Arrive in style in an electric vehicle, horse-drawn carriage or by tandem.

❋ **Clothes**: consider hiring outfits for groom and groomsmen. Some charities now run second-hand clothes stores specializing in wedding and bridesmaids' dresses.

❋ **Gifts**: have a wedding list at a green store or catalogue, or ask guests to contribute to your solar-panel fund. If you feel you have enough crockery and kitchen gadgets, choose a charity instead to receive donations in place of gifts for you.

❋ **Banquet**: Choose a caterer who can provide local, organic food and wine. Ask friends to bring a dessert.

142

April
30

Lovely Lather

Most commercial soaps for hand-washing dishes contain surfactants—the magic substance that cuts through grease. But surfactants are often made from petroleum, a finite resource, and therefore not a great idea to be washing them down your sink and into the water system.

Why not make your own dish soap? Collect those annoying little odds and ends of soap and once you have a handful, place in the bottom of a jar. Add hot water and mix—a jellylike substance should form. Spoon a little into the sink as you fill it to do the dishes. It will do the job perfectly well, and it's better for hands.

Sprinkle a little baking soda on messy pans and scrub—an ancient cleaning technique that does away with the need for any modern chemicals!

For a homemade concoction suitable for your dishwasher, add about a teaspoon of baking soda along with one of borax to the machine's soap dispenser.

If you are going to stick with buying dish-washing liquid, choose one made from vegetable oils, and perfume-free or a refillable eco-brand, reducing packaging too.

May
1

May Day/Beltane

On May 1, young girls used to rush out and wash their faces in the early morning dew, believing it had magic properties that would guarantee a beautiful complexion all year round. We may have dropped many of our old superstitions, but spring is still a magical time and worth celebrating.

Even today, England takes a step back in time on May Day. Village greens are covered with booths and fairs; men don straw hats and bells, the Morris dancers' traditional garb, to wind colorful ribbons around the maypole.

May Day harks back to a simpler time, more connected to the soil and seasons. Traditionally, it was a celebration of Beltane, the end of winter, and a time to look forward to planting and plenty in the summer months. The Romans had a similar festival in honor of Flora, their goddess of fruit and flowers.

May Day is also known as Garland Day, because people traditionally made beautiful garlands of seasonal greenery and flowers. And that's a simple and charming tradition that can be enjoyed the world over to mark the new season.

Down the Drain

It's obvious how much water you use when you take a bath. Imagine how many glasses of water that would be as you relax in all that drinking-quality water!

We use lots of water for washing ourselves, but being clean does not have to be the enemy of being green: simply follow the tips and guidelines in the panel below to minimize your impact.

For the very enthusiastic, consider showering and washing your hair a little less frequently to make real water savings. Put a bucket in the shower to collect water to recycle to wash the car or water the vegetable garden or your houseplants. Some rainwater-harvest schemes also produce fresh, clean water for washing.

Washing Wisely

✔ *Every minute you spend in the shower, gallons of water are being washed away, so keep it reasonably short.*

✔ *Fit a water-efficient shower head—most are so good that you won't feel the difference.*

✔ *Turn the tap off while you lather up, and on again to rinse.*

✔ *Save baths for a special, relaxing treat..*

✔ *And don't forget to cut down on the chemicals you pour down the drain and into the water system.*

May 3

Sharing the Ride

Many of us are used to thinking of our vehicle as our own personal kingdom, where we can choose the music, the temperature and direction of travel.

But when there's no alternative to owning a car, giving others a ride on a regular basis is a crucial way to help cut emissions and fuel use. Giving friends or colleagues a lift means at least they can leave their vehicle at home.

It can take a little planning, whether you informally ask others who might need to travel or join a community or workplace scheme that matches passengers and drivers for a more sociable, affordable and environmental way to travel.

In other car-share programs, members borrow a vehicle from

the organization whenever they need it. Members usually pay a fee to join and for usage, but it is a fraction of the cost of buying, insuring and maintaining your own vehicle. It suits people who only need a car once in a while, for example to collect bulky purchases or for a trip out of town.

Shop Intentionally

When you feel like your efforts are insignifcant drops in a great bucket, one place to remember you are powerful is right there in your pocket.

You can guarantee companies pay keen attention to how customers spend their money. Most are faster to respond to the bottom line than any number of eloquent letters and will be quick to develop green lines where they think it matters to consumers.

Buying organic or ethical products from your local superstore might encourage them to expand their range and make other shoppers aware of alternatives. Another, better way is to buy from smaller, local businesses.

You can also use your hard-earned cash to support the kinds of businesses you would like to see flourish—like local artisans or firms that give something back to the community or the planet.

The most important thing is to shop intentionally and thoughtfully, not simply pick the cheapest or most advertised brand. When you look down at your shopping basket full of sustainable, ethical goods, you will see a glimpse of the kind of world we want to live in.

May 5

The Humble Honeybee

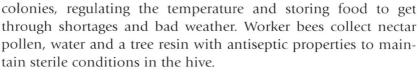

There's a lot we could learn from these amazing creatures. They live together in cooperative colonies, regulating the temperature and storing food to get through shortages and bad weather. Worker bees collect nectar pollen, water and a tree resin with antiseptic properties to maintain sterile conditions in the hive.

There are hundreds of different bee species, and not all produce honey or even sting. But they are crucially important pollinators, with a role to play in reproducing around one third of our food plants. Without bees to pollinate them in some areas, plant species are beginning to die out, changing the face of agriculture.

Bees are under threat. A lethal mite has been spreading through

colonies for more than two decades. Changing farming practices and damage to their habitats have also caused decimated populations, leaving a real possibility that this common insect could become extinct. It wouldn't just be a shame, but would have unknown consequences for our food production.

Compost Awareness Month

It seems nearly everything has an official international day, but compost is so rich and useful that it gets a whole month in the limelight!

Good compost needs air and moisture as well as a supply of nutritious food and garden waste to keep it well fed. Twigs, plain (unprinted) cardboard and egg shells all help to keep air pockets in your compost heap, so the helpful bugs get to work faster.

As you are building up your pile through the spring and summer months, turn it every so often with a garden fork. If it looks very dry, add a little water. Compost shouldn't smell; when it's ready it will have rotted down to about half the volume of what you put in, and it will look and smell like rich earth.

If you aren't already making compost, it's a great way to divert raw food waste, twigs and woody stems, leaves and cardboard from landfill and convert it into free fertilizer for your plants. Get an airtight container to collect your kitchen scraps and locate your compost bin away from the veggie patch but within easy reach of the back door. See February 17 to find out how to begin.

149

Call in a Favor

Working together often makes better use of our resources. Sometimes the green way of doing things can be a little more labor-intensive, like home improvement projects with fewer power tools. But getting a bunch of friends to come over and help makes it a social occasion.

Make sure you have all the supplies you need, and ask friends to bring paint brushes, tools or shovels from home. Remind them to wear old clothes too.

Compile a list of possible tasks and ensure everyone has the chance to rotate around jobs so they don't reach the point of boredom. Preparing a slap-up meal as a thank you will leave them with fond memories of the day. Be sure that you return the favor

whenever friends have a big job that needs doing with help too.

Sometimes we live in little pigeon holes, reluctant to intrude on other people's lives. But people are social creatures and often love to help out, lend their possessions and be part of a constructive team effort.

Breeze-dried Clothes

As the weather warms up, it's time to pull the plug on your clothes dryer. In fact, many households cope year round without one, making big savings to their carbon footprint and electricity bill.

Your clothes dryer is likely to be the second most costly home appliance to run (after the fridge) and produces a ton of carbon dioxide every year in the average household.

If you have outdoor space, you may well already be familiar with the special comfort of fresh, crisp, air-dried sheets and clothes. Rig up a good washing line or space-saving whirligig so you are ready to hang out whenever you need to.

Having plenty of places to hang clothes is key to drying the natural way. Inside, invest in a pulley or a freestanding clothes-drying rack (or clothes horse) that folds flat for easy storage and, for cooler days when you have the heating on, use radiator racks.

It will take a little longer to get your garments dry, but once you get in the habit, your household will be able to adjust quite easily to this much greener way of drying your clothes and you will feel the difference in your wallet too.

May
9

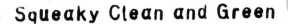

Squeaky Clean and Green

Our forefathers and -mothers made a lot more things for themselves, including soap.

The basic principles of traditional soap-making are simple—heating alkaline together with animal fat, cooling in molds and curing, allowing the soap to dry over the course of a few weeks.

In reality, though, the alkaline used in soap-making, known as lye, is a pretty hazardous substance, unpleasant to work with. If you have gloves, goggles, the equipment and expert advice, it can be a rewarding job, but otherwise, it can be a dangerous hobby.

An alternative is to buy the basic soap substance in bulk from a specialist supplier, ready to melt down and add your own finishing touch of scents, color and design. The advantage is that you

choose the additives, not the multinational toiletry company, so you can keep it simple and natural. Try the Soap-crafters site for more information, inspiration and supplies. Try collecting oddments of used soaps in a jar, add a little hot water and pour into a mold to set as a new bar. Soap oddments also deter moths, so keep them in your closets.

Home Energy Audit

Many of us are unaware of our home's biggest energy crimes. Where does all that heat go? Who's using all this electricity? As the world wakes up to dwindling fossil-fuel supplies and the need to curb carbon emissions, energy efficiency is the name of the game. Some energy companies and local authorities offer free energy audits for domestic properties and advice on how to cut energy use. Arrange a date, and even if you have had an audit in the past, take up the offer to find out how you are doing and what other savings you can make.

Lots of the recommended improvements are small and simple—you can install low-energy light bulbs quicker than you can say "rising sea levels." Other changes might be structural, particularly if you live in an older home. Winter is the time of highest heating costs, so now is the time to plan insulation and other important energy-saving projects.

Getting hold of a "smart meter" for a few days makes it easy for you and your family to see exactly how much electricity your gadgets use. Turn everything in the house off, then, one by one, switch all your usual appliances on and see how fast the units of electricity notch up. Suddenly, it's apparent that our homes use (and waste) a suprising amount of energy.

May 11

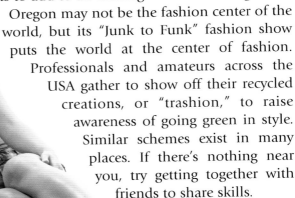

Customize Your Clothes

Is it a brave or foolish person who takes a pair of scissors to a perfectly good item of clothing? Well, it might be neither, if customizing older clothes—turning a dress into a skirt or making a sweater into a cute tank top—gives them a new lease of life and freshens up your wardrobe.

Simple changes include adding a belt, funky buttons or sequins. With no need for expert sewing skills, you can easily dye clothes.

Think through your project before starting, so that the end result is worthy of the Paris catwalks, not the fashion police. Pick up a couple of extra items from the bargain rail at the thrift store to practice on if you are unsure how to start, or simply cannibalize buttons, bows or fabric from worn garments to add to an existing item of clothing.

Oregon may not be the fashion center of the world, but its "Junk to Funk" fashion show puts the world at the center of fashion. Professionals and amateurs across the USA gather to show off their recycled creations, or "trashion," to raise awareness of going green in style. Similar schemes exist in many places. If there's nothing near you, try getting together with friends to share skills.

Green Car Washing

No matter how much you love your car, it doesn't need to be rinsed in water fit for drinking! Getting the car clean can be done without wasteful water use.

It might be worth asking whether it really needs a full-scale wash before you begin. When you can no longer tell your vehicle's color, the answer is yes, but often a quick wipe of windows and lights will do just as well as washing the whole thing.

Use a bucket, sponge and a little elbow grease to get the dirt off rather than a hose, which will use much more water. You could even put the bucket in the shower to fill with water that would otherwise drain away, or use rainwater from your garden water butt, thereby using water that hasn't been treated.

Even better, wash your car on the lawn, so that it gets a sprinkling at the same time.

As with other cleaning challenges, avoid toxic chemicals and look for a natural, vegetable-based product and use a nonabrasive, but tough, cleaning cloth.

Some environmentalists argue it's better to use a commercial car wash, where the mucky water is treated rather than just flushed down the drain as is. If you choose a commercial wash, go for one that recycles the rinse water.

May 13

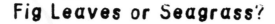

Fig Leaves or Seagrass?

A group of women got together in 2006 to enjoy a weekend of yoga and kayaking. Paddling on the Indian River Lagoon on Florida's eastern coast, they were shocked to see how pollution and a large number of motorized boats were wrecking this fragile marine environment.

The lagoon, with its shallow waters, mangroves and seagrass beds, is the perfect habitat for osprey, dolphins, and hundreds of fish and plant species. But since 1950, one-third of the seagrass had been destroyed. The women felt determined to do something.

Inspired by the English Women's Institute members who bared almost all for a fundraising calendar (inspiring the movie *Calendar Girls*), they decided to take the plunge for this natural treasure.

They made their own revealing calendar, "The Lagoon Can't Bare it Alone," raising $12,000 for local organizations protecting the wetland. March was also declared seagrass awareness month for all of Florida.

All it took was a little guts, imagination and teamwork for these proactive women to make a difference.

For the Birds

Around now, millions of birds are on the move from their winter homes, and their return is a sign that summer is well on its way in the northern hemisphere. International Migratory Bird Day, held on the second Saturday in May, celebrates their extraordinary annual journeys.

In the Americas, 350 species of birds make the trek from their nesting grounds in the north to spend the winter where food is plentiful in the American South, Southwest and Mexico and the Caribbean. A particularly intrepid traveler is the arctic tern, which travels between the Arctic Circle and Antarctica.

Migratory birds are vital to the natural cycles of the world, but changing climate patterns are playing havoc with their routes, habitats and food supplies. Human activities like hunting have taken their toll; building power lines and wind farms disrupt the migrants' flyways (like a bird highway but with fewer signposts).

Treaties were signed early in the last century, committing the USA, Canada, Japan, Mexico and Russia to work together to protect around 800 species of migratory birds on their journey.

Find out more about migratory birds at www.birdday.org.

May 15

Veggie Boxes

If you struggle to eat the recommended daily amount of fruit and veggies, or to source enough fresh, locally grown produce, then a farm's veggie-box scheme could solve all your woes in one fell swoop.

A box of tasty vegetables, sometimes with home-baked bread or farm-made cheese, is delivered to your door. The contents depend on what's in season, so you know it's as fresh as can be. Most supply only local vegetables and fruits; some include fairtrade goods.

Vegetable-box schemes are usually run by farmers or small co-ops, so you are cutting out the middle man and often getting a bargain too. Your delivery will come in a box that is returned empty, so there is little or no packaging.

It might seem daunting to take delivery of a surprising box of seasonal produce each week or two, but it's a great incentive for trying new recipes and is bound to lead to some delicious culinary adventures.

Ask local producers or at farmers' markets to find a local scheme, or encourage them to start one.

May 16

The Problem with Landfill

Hands up who wants to live next to a massive mound of garbage? On a much larger scale, that's what we are all doing. Megatons of waste are dumped in holes in the ground each year. It's like sweeping all our festering garbage under the carpet and hoping it just goes away.

Not only are cities running out of room for landfill, but the dumps are major environmental hazards, giving off methane fumes and toxic run-off as rain trickles through the cocktail of materials.

To make matters worse, much of what goes to landfill could be put to perfectly good use. Electrical goods, textiles, scrap metal and building materials could all still have a useful life. Things no longer of use can be disposed of in a more useful way—such as using them for parts or recycling them. Food can be composted so the nutrients go back into the soil to help something else grow.

To cut down on landfill, we need to throw less stuff out, reducing waste and extending the lifespan of the things we own. Then we need to get smart about how we dispose of what's left. But to get to the root of the problem, we need to use fewer of our resources to begin with.

DO IT!

159

May 17

Quality Pays

It's hard to beat the excitement of finding a bargain, but our obsession with cheap goods isn't doing the planet any favors. Why buy cheap appliances or household goods if you're only going to have to throw them out and then make the same shopping trip in another year or two?

When making a purchase, ask yourself how long you expect the item to last. Then think about the cost spread out over the total number of years. A bargain brand of cheap carpet that will last only a year or two may not compare so well with a more expensive, higher-quality product that might last you a lifetime.

Quality is not the same as expensive, of course, but reputable brands that come with a lengthy warranty can be a good sign that the item is built to last. Ask friends or search consumer websites for recommendations too.

Second-hand goods can be a good option for household goods, clothes and furniture: not only will you save a pretty penny, but you can see how well they withstand regular use.

Pedal Power

Cycling could just be the perfect way to travel—it's virtually free, you can whiz past traffic jams, and parking problems will become a thing of the past. Regular adult cyclists also acquire the fitness level of a person ten years younger, and your bicycle creates no pollution.

If you haven't cycled since childhood, this is a great time of year get back on your bike—and cycling is a skill you don't forget!

Second-hand and refurbished bicycles are reasonably priced, but you will need to invest in a decent lock, a safety helmet and reflective jacket, and bright night lights if you don't have them yet.

If you feel nervous, start pedaling on designated cycle routes and quiet roads for fun until you build up your confidence. Alternatively, an organized bike trek will get you in shape and on track, with someone else taking care of all the practicalities.

Once you are up and pedaling, think about what journeys you regularly make—to work, the gym, or shopping—that could be done by bike. Research good routes, avoiding heavy traffic where possible. You will also find there is something of a fraternity among fellow cyclists who will be happy to give you pointers.

May 19

Sundials

Although they may seem old-fashioned now, sundials are the most ancient device for telling time, and among our oldest scientific instruments. The first sundials relied on the position of the sun to divide the day into hours, although because of the earth's wobble on its axis, summer hours were longer than winter hours, so they were not precise.

There are more types of sundial than there are time zones in the world. The first sundials we know of were the Egyptian obelisks of tall, narrow stone; the oldest surviving sundial is around 3,000 years old. The Greeks improved and expanded upon the earlier designs, but hour length continued to vary with the season. It was not until the Arab mathematician Ibn al-Shatir realized that the

gnomon (the straight bit) had to be parallel with the earth's axis that sundials began to display hours of equal length year-round.

If you want to make your own sundial, there is plenty of advice online. Just remember that the sun itself doesn't observe Daylight Savings Time, so your clock and your sundial won't always agree.

Natural Weed Control

When your beautiful garden is overrun with weeds, it might be tempting to reach for the most toxic weedkiller you can find, but resist! Chemicals designed to poison tough weeds will do no favors to your plants, soil, insects and animals in your garden or, indeed, human beings.

Weeds are a definitely a problem, depriving the plants we want to grow of space, light and nutrients. In winter months, weeds on the vegetable patch can be better for your earth than leaving it bare, but they need to be pulled or dug in before you can start planting. A simple solution is to cover the ground with a piece of old carpet or plastic sheeting until you are ready for spring.

The old-fashioned way of identifying and pulling weeds by hand or with a hoe is an organic alternative to chemical sprays. Make sure to take the roots with them or they'll be back.

After you have weeded, a layer of mulch around the base of your plants helps keep weeds at bay.

Young weeds can be put on the compost heap, but make sure they are cut before they produce seeds (ie, when still in flower), or the seeds will thrive in the rich nitrogen of the compost heap, guaranteeing years of future weeding.

May 21

Love Your Library

If the word "library" conjures up a picture of dusty rows of books and overbearing librarians, ticking readers off for the slightest cough, then it's probably a long while since you set foot in one.

Libraries are an amazing resource for the community and for the person seeking to live more greenly. In most cases, we don't need to own a personal copy of a book to enjoy it, and fewer copies mean fewer trees cut down and less energy to produce them.

If you are heading on vacation, check out the guide books and maps available for loan—it saves the trouble of buying a book just for a week. You can also use the collections as a trial to see which recipe or hobby books are really worth purchasing for yourself.

Many public libraries now offer CDs and movies, and if there's a charge, it's generally much lower than the video store. Borrowing stuff is just the tip of the iceberg—some libraries have cafés, internet access and a wealth of lectures and special events.

So join your local library, make the most of its facilities, and don't forget… shhh!

May 22

Biodiversity Day

Today is International Biodiversity Day, celebrating the wondrous diversity of the natural world.

In 1992, a large number of nations signed a convention recognizing that we are all part of the web of life and, in fact, depend on its richness and variety. Leaders agreed to work together to stop the loss of ecosystems, plants and animals, because preserving the diversity of life on earth is essential to our own survival.

Through changes in the way we deal with waste, agriculture and trade, they set tough targets that were designed to halt the decline in biodiversity by 2010.

Almost every country on the planet has signed up; at the time of writing the United States had not yet ratified the treaty but has taken steps to implement its measures.

It seems obvious that people rely on a healthy, thriving environment, and that protecting it is in our own interests as well. It's a shame that sometimes it takes the world leaders a while longer to attend to the important issues, but at least this day keeps biodiversity in the spotlight once a year.

For more on this topic, see the Convention on Biological Diversity site.

May
23

Amazing Microbes

You may never have seen them or even be aware of their existence, but tiny soil microbes are essential to the plants, flowers and vegetables growing in our gardens, parks and fields. These microscopic bacteria and fungi help break down organic matter, recycling nutrients back into the soil to help healthy new plants to grow and thrive.

Left to their own devices, the microbes will chomp through the rich nitrogen in bark, leaves and seeds on a forest floor in around five years. In our gardens, though, we harness the might of microbes in the compost heap, to speed up the process of getting newly available nutrients out of our garden and kitchen waste.

As the single-celled beings get busy with food scraps and garden waste, they use up oxygen in the composter and create heat. Your compost heap works harder in the summer.

You don't need to get personally acquainted with the little guys, but remembering they like warmth, air and a little moisture will make your compost bin a much more hospitable place for their valuable work.

Dry Gardening

In the hot New Mexico summer, half of all house-hold water use is outside, much of it in the garden. In all kinds of climates, many of us are all too familiar with managing the garden during hosepipe and sprinkler bans, when water is in short supply. As the climate changes, this will only become more frequent and occur in more and more places.

When choosing plants for your garden, avoid very thirsty ones that need lots of extra water in the warmer months. Limit the area of lawn (or do without it if your climate doesn't support grass naturally) and don't trim the grass too short: it will dry out very fast.

Adding a layer of compost or mulch (a layer of decomposing organic material, like leaves, grass cuttings or weeds) to your flowerbeds and veggie garden helps the ground to stay moist.

When you do need to add extra water, do so in the early morning or in the evening, when there will be less evaporation. Use a can to water the base of dry plants rather than a sprinkler, which will spray water everywhere indiscriminately.

Finally, install a water butt or use waste water from the shower or washing vegetables rather than potable water.

May 25

Bottled Water

Bottled water from a Swiss glacier sounds very refreshing, healthy and pure, but every single plastic bottle has a huge environmental footprint.

There's the packaging, industrial extraction, miles of travel and the questionable claim that what's in the bottle is better than what's in the tap. The Polaris Institute in Canada found that some big companies simply draw water from normal public supplies.

Americans drink their way through 30 billion bottles of water each year. Manufacturing a standard plastic bottle can use seven times as much water as the final product can hold. Even if bottles are recycled (and the majority are not), the recycling process uses much more water and energy than providing public piped water.

To cap it all, bottled water costs hundreds of times more than a glass from the faucet.

Invest in a bottle you can refill and take it with you when you are on the move. Ask for tap water in restaurants and cafes, and if you have to buy a bottle, choose the local brand.

Cashing in on Cans

It can seem a little bit of a hassle to rinse out and recycle tin cans, but it's a massive energy saver when you consider that recycling one uses just 5 percent of the energy of extracting raw materials to make a brand new one.

As people become more deliberate and conscientious about recycling, and with a big market for second-generation materials, there's money to be made too. Sometimes recyclers will pay for your old cans, to ensure a supply of their raw material.

One woman put her "can-do" attitude to work in aid of her local church. Sue Scott collected, sorted and sold 140,000 cans for recycling to raise £900 (more than $1200) for a new ladder to the Groby Parish Church tower and repairs to the old bells.

Why not give your workplace, school or community group the recycling bug by organizing a fundraising can collection? Find a company that will buy them from you, somewhere to store them and a good cause. Set a target for extra motivation and watch the cans roll in. When you have collected your quota, haul them to the recycling plant for the payoff, for you, the cause and the planet.

Trash to Treasure

Garage sales, yard sales—call them what you will, they are a fantastic way of clearing out old things and earning a little cash, as are online alternatives. Or picking up some new-to-you items at a fraction of the cost. Whether you are buying or selling, this is a great way to keep useful items out of landfill and cut consumption of new materials.

The first step is venturing to the back of closets and the attic, sorting through clothes, household items, books and records for things you no longer need. Try to resist the temptation of holding onto something in case you find a use for it one day—better give it a good home with someone who wants to use it today.

If your children are outgrowing their toys and clothes or you

need to free up shelf space, go for a themed sale and invite relevant customers—young families, or bookworms, say.

Go it alone, inviting buyers to your place on the designated day, or join an organized event, where you can bring a table or car full of stuff to sell for a small fee.

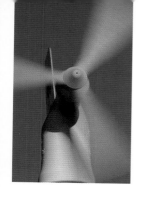

Micro-Generation

Water and wind are at their strongest in the winter months, when it's coldest and we need energy to heat and light our homes. It's almost as if nature intended us to harness these power sources for renewable, reliable energy!

As the name suggests, micro-generation is producing small amounts of power close to where it's needed. When electricity is transferred along power lines, a certain amount is lost.

A growing number of people are doing it, but don't imagine a mini-power station on your front lawn. If your home is on a suitable site, a solar panel or geothermal system will be barely noticeable, while a domestic wind turbine is pretty compact. And if your personal castle comes with its own stream, river or waterfall, even a small hydro project is also a possibility!

The initial outlay can be considerable for some of these options, but most schemes will pay for themselves over the years as you generate some of your power for free from carbon-neutral sources. Some financial support might be available, and you should invite a renewable energy engineer to advise on the best options for your property.

May 29

No More "Soup in a Cube"

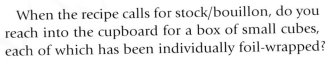

When the recipe calls for stock/bouillon, do you reach into the cupboard for a box of small cubes, each of which has been individually foil-wrapped?

Basic broth or stock is one of those fantastic, old-fashioned ingredients we have almost forgotten how to make. An essential ingredient in soups, stews and risottos, it's free to make and will help get every last ounce of flavor and goodness out of your grocery basket. Sure, it takes a little more planning than the powdered kind, but once made, you can simply freeze it in small containers.

Taking Stock

As you are preparing any homemade dishes with fresh vegetables, put to one side the peelings, onion layers and seeds (all the scraps, except the green parts on potatoes and anything from a chilli). Store in a bag or box in the freezer until you have accumulated around two cups. Then add to your saucepan with a couple of pints of water, a little salt and cumin and boil for about 30 minutes. Hey presto, beautiful bouillon!

Freshen Up

Most commercial air fresheners mask smells with artificial, chemical scents rather than doing anything to restore air quality or cleanliness. And when you think about the average family, which buys 36 air fresheners each year, that's a lot of chemicals inhaled and packaging used up.

Avoid products containing parfum and artificial musk, which can cause respiratory irritation, and any aerosols. Better still, give up on canned fresh air and use these natural (and virtually free) ways to breathe better, cleaner, fresher air indoors.

A Breath of Fresh Air

- ✔ *Open a window: the fresh breeze will get stale air moving.*
- ✔ *A bowl of white vinegar or hot water with a squeeze of lemon left in a room for an hour will deodorize the atmosphere.*
- ✔ *Hang curtains and carpets outside on a dry day to air, and beat them with a tennis racket if they are musty or stale.*
- ✔ *Baking soda is a natural odor-absorber. Use in the garbage can, the fridge, or sprinkle on carpets and vacuum off.*
- ✔ *Maintain healthy pot plants to improve air quality.*
- ✔ *To add your own natural scents, use dried flowers, lavender, dried citrus peel, pine cones or essential oils.*

May 31

Willow

Willow's fast-growing branches and strong, vigorous roots make it a most useful plant. Medicines, cricket bats, building material, basketwork—it would be quicker to mention what it has not been used for than what you can do with this versatile wood. And where would we be without aspirin, a drug originally based on the acids found in the plant's bark?

Nature too has found countless uses for these beautiful trees. They are an important food source for bees and moths, and, growing on river banks, the trees prevent soil erosion. It's no wonder the willow tree has featured in centuries of folklore.

Willow is native to the northern hemisphere's temperate regions. Strong, slender one-year-old branches called osiers are

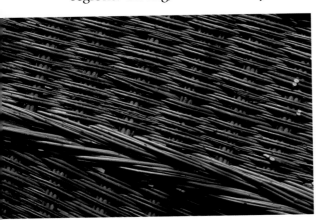

used for basket and wicker work. Its fast growth rate and high energy content make it a renewable energy source, usually burned for heat with charcoal as a byproduct.

If you want to add a willow to your garden, most varieties grow well from cuttings.

Shall I compare thee to a summer's day?
Thou art more lovely and more temperate:
Rough winds do shake the darling buds of May,
And summer's lease hath all too short a date:
Sometime too hot the eye of heaven shines,
And often is his gold complexion dimmed,
And every fair from fair sometime declines,
By chance, or nature's changing course untrimmed:
But thy eternal summer shall not fade,
Nor lose possession of that fair thou ow'st,
Nor shall death brag thou wander'st in his shade,
When in eternal lines to time thou grow'st,
So long as men can breathe, or eyes can see,
So long lives this, and this gives life to thee.

—Sonnet 18
William Shakespeare

Stores Unwrapped

Supermarket bosses just love packaging—they think all the bright colors make us buy more. But customers and the planet are paying the price for the fancy wrappings on groceries—most of it ends up getting thrown away.

There are stores out there whose management staff aim to take the packaging out of produce: you bring your own containers and fill up just as much as you want. They are run by local food co-ops, whole food stores and, increasingly, trendy eco-boutiques.

The store buys in bulk and keeps food in sealed containers or dispensers, so that there are no hygiene worries. You can transfer your purchases straight to your own containers, ready to store at home. Best of all, packaging waste becomes a thing of the past.

You can also take the initiative to reduce the packaging when you are dealing with small, eco-minded shops and producers. Bring back your egg cartons, jars, potato sacks, paper and shopping bags when you're out replenishing supplies at the farmers' market or grocery store.

Transition Towns

The world over, small communities are preparing for the day when we run out of the readily accessible oil that is in easy-to-process forms. "Transition Towns" are working out how their communities can thrive without relying on fossil fuels. Oil products are ubiquitous: the "liquid gold" is a component of all kinds of household items, including sneakers, lycra, glue, plastic bottles, DVDs, contact lenses, computers and shoe polish. We have used up vast reserves of it and will soon face dwindling supplies, turning our economy upside down.

From Boulder, Colorado, to Canterbury, England, and El Manzano in Chile, communities are taking positive action to address the challenges this situation poses. They plan to reduce their energy consumption over a period of about fifteen years, with grassroots working groups looking at sustainable, post-Peak Oil options for food, homes and transportation. These aren't fringe groups, but concerned citizens who recognize the need for urgent change.

The Transition Network offers lots of support and ideas about how to get a whole town working together for a sustainable future. For more information, see the Transition Towns website or consult *The Transition Handbook*.

June 3

Natural Air Conditioning

When it's hot and sticky, it's almost too much to find the energy to flick on the AC. But that's when you home starts guzzling energy, and there are various low-energy steps you can take as an alternative, or else to cut down on how much you use the air conditioning.

Keeping your house cool is about blocking, removing and reducing heat. Prevent sunlight streaming into rooms that face the sun, using shades or something shiny or white that reflects heat away. Create a through draft, as the moving air will feel less stifling. Place a frozen bottle of water in front of an electric fan for a cooling effect using a fraction of the power.

If you live in a climate with long, hot summers, smart building is the best way to keep your home cool. Overhanging eaves,

awnings, shutters, shade trees outside windows, or blinds or drapes all help block the sun and reduce heat build-up.

If you really need an AC system, choose a low-energy model, make sure it is properly fitted, without leaks and turn it on sparingly to cool one or two rooms rather than the whole house.

Clean Air Day

Today, Canada marks Clean Air Day. It's a shame to have to get out to the countryside to breathe fresh, clean air, though that's a reality for many city dwellers.

While black clouds of smog are a thing of the past in most Western cities, airborne particles and noxious gases from industry, power stations and traffic fumes are often invisible. They are particularly nasty, as we inhale them straight into our lungs. These pollutants can cause irritation to eyes, breathing difficulties and an increased risk of lung disease, asthma and heart attack. Anyone can be affected, but children are particularly vulnerable.

Air quality also has a huge impact on entire natural cycles. Sulphur dioxide and nitrogen oxide cause clouds to become acidic. When acid rain falls, it damages fish, forests and more. This problem is particularly devastating in Canada, as the water cycle doesn't include natural filtering through lime or other rocks that can help counteract the acidity.

Tighter pollution controls have helped to tackle some emissions, like lead from vehicle fuel. But at the same time, our appetite for energy and travel has grown. Air quality is yet another reason to reduce our energy consumption.

June 5

World Environment Day

We can't confine caring about the environment to just one day, but the United Nations' World Environment Day provides a global focus for raising awareness and taking action. And it's one of the oldest annual celebrations of all things environmental, dating back to 1972.

Bringing together declarations by heads of state with local street parties and school activities, this observance is a chance for combined action on a common theme. In 2008, for example, the focus of the day was how to kick the CO_2 habit.

In 2007, Cameroon's University of Yaounde planted trees and put on drama performances to highlight the effects of environmental change. In 2004, plastic bag recycling was introduced to every school in the Cayman Islands.

Today is a chance to connect with people in far-flung parts of the globe and work alongside them for positive change. Plenty of ideas can be found on the UN Environment Programme website, and you can find out what's happening in your country. So what will you do today?

Wholesome Oats

A wholesome, delicious bowl of granola and fruit is the perfect way to start the day, but you don't need to rely on the store-bought variety. Better still, you can make it exactly the way you like it, whether you are nuts about raisins or can't stand picking out pumpkin seeds. Master the basic recipe and then experiment. Store the end result in an airtight container and serve with your homemade yogurt (see April 27).

Oats are an excellent source of fiber and protein and are low in cholesterol and saturated fat. Whether in the form of porridge or granola, whole oats provide an unbeatable breakfast.

Homemade Granola

Mix in a bowl ⅓ cup of vegetable oil, ⅓ cup of honey (or maple syrup, or a mixture of the two), ⅓ cup of skimmed milk (optional), 1 teaspoon of vanilla, 1 teaspoon of cinnamon and a pinch of salt. Then add five cups of rolled oats and mix well. You can add a little desiccated coconut if you like it. Spread the mixture over a baking tray and bake at 375°F (190°C) until golden brown, or about 10–15 minutes. Then comes the fun part! After cooling, add whichever of the following ingredients you like: almonds, pecans, walnuts, hazelnuts, raisins, dried cranberries, chopped dried apricots, dried banana, coconut flakes, sunflower seeds, pine kernels or pumpkin seeds. Store in an airtight container.

June 7

World Oceans Day

Today's the day to celebrate our oceans, whether you live on an island and see the sea every day or in the midst of the desert and have never cast eyes on open water.

Oceans cover three-quarters of the Earth's surface and were home to the very first life on our planet. They remain intimately connected to almost everything we need to live and thrive. They help to cool the planet and regulate our weather, and they help to generate the oxygen we breathe and the water we drink. The ocean is also home to many marine plants and creatures, from microscopic plankton through coral and seaweed to mammoth whales.

As well as the natural properties, we derive great pleasure from swimming, surfing on the waves, beachcombing or looking out at gorgeous sunsets over the water—who can put a price on that!

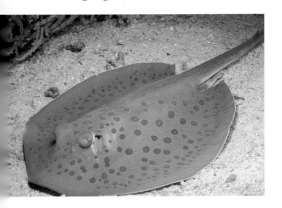

But our relationship with the oceans has not always been a two-way street. Our pollution ends up in the seas, and many fish species have been exploited.

World Oceans Day is the perfect opportunity for a beach trip. Or, if that's too far, visit an aquarium or else sign up for a campaign to clean up the oceans or enforce sustainable fishing practices.

Keeping Chickens

You've planted the veggie garden and baked your own bread: now you're feeling ready for the next step. How about keeping your own chickens, if you have space?

If you live in an urban area, it's wise to check local laws and conditions on your land to ensure that you are allowed. Get a decent book on raising poultry, so you can keep them healthy and happy. Bear in mind that they are a commitment: they need to be let out of their henhouse at dawn and locked in again at dusk every day, to protect them from predators, whether in urban or rural settings.

Chicks can be purchased direct from a supplier. Opt for heritage breeds if you can, because many are in danger of dying out as commercial farms prefer fast-growing varieties.

Alternatively, you might choose fully grown rescue chickens, formerly in the battery sector. One charity, the Battery Hen Welfare Trust, has recooped 120,000 birds with families and smallholders. They'll look sickly when they arrive, from a year of living in cramped conditions, but most will recover with time.

With a little room for them to roam and a simple coop, you'll soon be getting your own nutritious free-range eggs, while the chicken manure will also give the garden a boost if you add it to your compost heap.

June 9

Magnificent Madagascar

The world's fourth-largest island, Madagascar lies off the south-eastern coast of Africa. It boasts an almost unrivaled ecological richness. Around 5 percent of all the plant and animal species in the world live on this island, which is smaller than Texas, and many of these diverse species are found nowhere else on the face of the planet.

The island's forests are home to the baobab, or "upside-down tree," the national tree, among the many native species in the island's tropical dry forests. Medicine men have used plants from here for centuries in curative rituals, and many more modern remedies originate in these forests, too.

The island's wildlife includes 75 species of lemurs, a relative of the mongoose, the fossa and little shrewlike tenrecs. Unfortunately, many animal species have died out since humans arrived, including ten-foot tall elephant birds, giant lemurs and dwarf Malagasy hippopotamuses.

Further extinctions are a real possibility, as many of the country's animals are on the endangered list.

Office Staples

They are so small that we take these useful items for granted. They bind magazines, hold our papers in order and prevent complete chaos reigning on desks and in offices throughout the world. But every staple is made from a tiny nugget of metal that cannot be easily reused or recycled.

If every administrator, office worker, teacher and committee secretary used just one fewer staple each day, literally thousands of tons of metal would be saved over the course of a year. The huge numbers of those little metal strips all add up.

When papers need to held together temporarily, try finding a re-usable alternative to staples, like a paper clip. For filing purposes, invest in recycled cardboard folders, which can hold your paperwork together but also be readily reused (or recycled) when it's time to reorganize and update your records.

For no more than the cost of a regular stapler, you can buy a stapleless alternative, which folds a little corner of paper in an ingeniously simple way, so documents stay together. As a bonus, you never need to worry about running out of staples again—or, for that matter, stapling your thumb!

June
11

Summer Seasonals

As the garden yields its first crops of the summer, it's not hard to eat seasonal foods at this time of the year. Enjoy fresh peas and beans, aromatic tomatoes and delicious, juicy strawberries at the right time of the year and it becomes apparent that those air-freighted, out-of-season alternatives may look tempting, but taste like cardboard by comparison.

We've all been looking forward to the luscious summer fruits that will ripen this month and later on in the season—raspberries, redcurrants, cherries, plums and more. If you grow your own and you have more fruit than you can eat fresh, or give to friends, it's time to begin your jam-making and to restock the kitchen with delicious preserves, dried fruits and chutneys for the year ahead.

On hot days, make fresh salads of lettuce, tomatoes and peppers. Enjoy seasonal vegetables at their best, soon after picking. If

you aren't able to grow your own, it's the best time to frequent the farmers' market, where the produce will have been picked that morning in the local farms. See June 29 for more on preserving seasonal foods to enjoy later.

Our Wriggly Friends

There are thousands of worm varieties, wriggling their way though virtually every habitat on planet Earth. But our particular common garden species, the earthworm, is a very useful and helpful creature.

Worms help to turn the soil in our gardens, aerate it and keep it in good condition for growing things. Encourage earthworms in your garden by avoiding the use of chemical fertilizers and weed killers (which can destroy them), and use plenty of natural mulch.

If you don't have room for a compost container, you can harness the power of worms to turn food scraps into nutritious plant food. You can mail-order tiger worms or red worms with a modest-sized container for your veggie peelings, which, to its new residents, resembles a luxury condo with several floors.

The worms will make their way through most vegetable scraps (but not meat, citrus, onion, garlic or potatoes) and small amounts of paper and leaves, giving off a waste liquid you can collect via a tap at the base of the wormery. Water it down and use as a nutritious plant food. You will get very rich compost, suitable for use as potting compost to give seeds a good start in life.

June 13

Bottle Banking

Glass was one of the first materials to be widely recycled, because it can be melted down and used many times without deteriorating. And it makes a big difference: recycling two bottles saves enough energy to make five hot drinks.

It's best if glass is sorted into different colors before recycling—those new green bottles hanging on the wall can only be made from old green or clear glass. Where glass colors are mixed for recycling, the resulting glass will be brown.

Old glass can also be used to make tableware, processed sand for building and other purposes (so no need to remove more from the beach),and to make bricks and road-surfacing materials. Make sure to buy recycled glass products too.

Ten Green Bottles

In Denmark, more than 99 percent of glass Carlsberg beer bottles are returned intact to the plant for washing and refilling, thanks to a deposit scheme that gives bar owners and drinkers a small cash refund for every one. Each bottle is used an estimated 33 times before being melted down and recycled.

The Bottomless Cart

Most families could cut their grocery bill by a third if they could buy just what was needed, get the quantities right when cooking and reduce the amount that ends up going to waste. Those potential savings make a little extra planning well worth doing: you'll soon notice the difference.

Before you even leave the house, check what you have in and write a list of what you need to buy. A menu plan for the week ahead will make sure you have everything you need—and nothing you don't. At the grocery store, follow the plan. It's fine to buy canned and dry foods in bulk (and you might cut down on packaging if you do so), but resist succumbing to sale prices and offers on fresh foods that will go uneaten.

When you get home, make sure the foods you bought are stored properly for freshness and to make sure they last. Even long-life store cupboard staples will benefit from airtight containers.

It's worth learning how much your family usually eats of particular foods. Make the effort to measure or think about quantities when you're cooking, rather than guessing. See January 17 and December 26 for leftovers and other food-saving suggestions.

June 15

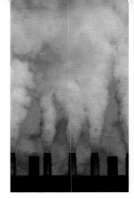

Carbon Offsets

Among the new industries springing up around the climate-change challenge are carbon-offsetting firms. When you take part in activities that produce carbon emissions, you can buy an offset: for a small fee, the company undertakes projects to reduce the emissions, like planting trees.

It's an attractive idea—too attractive, say some campaigners. They believe what you really purchase is a conscience salve, allowing you continue your carbon-wasteful lifestyle without making changes. Such schemes can create a "carbon neutral" veneer, while the neutralizing projects are long-term and may happen anyway.

But fans argue that it helps put a price on emitting carbon for businesses concerned with the bottom line, and for consumers,

who become more aware of the environmental costs of their choices. Offsetting companies must publish details of how they reduce emissions and are independently audited.

At the end of the day, it's possible to offset our carbon emissions with such schemes at the same time as working to reduce them.

Best-dressed Burgers

Where would we be without the burger's best friend, tomato ketchup? Our organic beefburger in a home-made bun just wouldn't taste the same without it. If you and your family love ketchup, why not try making your own? Without additives or artificial preservatives, it's a worthy condiment for any outdoor feast, and it's always popular with the kids.

This recipe will keep refrigerated for about two to three weeks, or preserved in sterilized, sealed jars for up to a year.

Tomato Ketchup

1 can of whole tomatoes, pureed, or 2 lbs fresh tomatoes, chopped
1 chopped onion
1 tablespoon of olive oil
1 tablespoon of tomato paste
1 teaspoon brown sugar
¾ cup vinegar
pinch salt
Spices: 1 to 2 teaspoons of combination of cayenne pepper, cinnamon, cloves, allspice; or use whole versions in a muslin bag.
Sauté the onion until soft. Add tomatoes and other ingredients. Simmer for about an hour, stirring occasionally until the mixture thickens. Remove spice bag, if using. Puree in a blender or simply push through a sieve, then allow to cool before serving or bottling.

June 17

Creeping Deserts

The World Day to Combat Desertification highlights the urgent need to arrest the process by which land becomes degraded and dry until it is a hostile desert. Deserts cover one third of the Earth's land, but they are spreading quickly as a result of climate factors and human activities.

Nonsustainable farming strips the land of nutrients and can leave it barren. Cutting down trees leaves the earth vulnerable to erosion by wind and rain. Drought also plays a part.

It's poor farmers and herders who suffer when the lands that provided their food and livelihood turn to desert. As much as a fifth of the world's population is in areas at risk of desertification.

You don't need to be Lawrence of Arabia to know that deserts are pretty hostile environments. Without foliage to absorb some

heat, equatorial deserts experience soaring temperatures by day and extreme cold at night. Cold deserts experience low temperatures with drought conditions.

The good news is that the degradation of land can be reversed—but only if we act in time.

Natural Pest Control

Before declaring chemical warfare on the caterpillars and slugs that are eating their way through your vegetable patch, it's worth trying the host of organic ways of deterring and removing pests. Whenever you have an invasion or plant disease, seek out natural ways of dealing with it.

One of the best ways of keeping your garden pest-free is to encourage pest-controlling creatures. Feed the birds in winter and you will be rewarded in the summer months as they return to nibble on destructive pests in your garden.

Encourage frogs and toads, hungry insect-eaters, by leaving areas of long grass and shade. Centipedes, ground beetles, lacewing, spiders and ladybugs are all friendly bugs that help to keep the more damaging kinds at bay.

Planting the same vegetable in the same spot year after year may allow pests or disease to take hold, so rotate crops around the vegetable patch and use companion planting (see March 28) to harness the power of plants against pests.

Don't forget the simple steps, like a solid fence, which will prevent dogs, cats and possibly rabbits from destroying your prize cauliflowers.

Bat Basics

Their night-time antics and association with Halloween don't exactly put bats at the top of the "cute and cuddly animals to protect" table. But the thousand species of bat, many of which are under threat, are important.

Far from their blood-sucking image—Count Dracula has a lot of answer for—many bats eat only fruits and seeds. They fly further than many other propagators, helping to spread and strengthen fruit crops. Others eat insects, keeping their populations at bay. Both fruit-bats and insect eaters play a vital role in agriculture.

Many ecosystems that once supported bats have been destroyed. Some try to find nooks and crannies in buildings to roost in. Put a bat box in your garden to provide a safe place for them to live.

If you find an injured bat, don't pick it up, but call a local animal sanctuary, as there is a chance of rabies infection. Bats can live for more than twenty years, so attempting a rescue is worth it.

Did You Know?

Far from being "blind as a bat," many species have excellent eye-sight adapted to low light conditions. They navigate by echolocation: sending out sonar signals that bounce off objects and return to their large ears.

Specs Sense

When your eyesight changes, there's no need to hang on to your old glasses. Especially not when they can be recycled to make a new pair for someone who can't afford to buy their own. If you wear glasses, you will know yourself how difficult life would be without being able to see properly —reading, driving and working pose real challenges.

Vision Aid Overseas is one charity refurbishing old glasses to go to those who need them—over 300,000 pairs have been distributed so far. They are sorted, cleaned, distributed and eventually matched to the eyesight needs of patients in developing countries.

Such projects are also keeping all those valuable materials out of landfill and giving your old horn-rimmed specs a new lease of life. Next time you replace your glasses, ask your opticians if they collect old ones for recycling or redistribution.

If the frames of your old glasses are still in good condition, consider holding on to them and replacing only the lenses with your new prescription. They'll cost less to renew and keep the old frames in use for longer.

June 21

Midsummer's Eve

There is a long tradition of marking the summer solstice, the longest day of the year, though because of calendar changes it no longer falls exactly on this day.

Among other ancient cultures that celebrated light and life at this time, it was a major Celtic festival: it's still marked in Ireland with fairs, festivals, fireworks and bonfires. Traditionally, herbs and medicinal plants were gathered before sunrise on the solstice, as it was believed their healing powers were at their height.

The Celts were intimately connected with the world around them and worshipped the forces of nature. They believed elements of the natural world contained spirits, so that every mountain,

river, tree and spring was seen as sacred. It made them reluctant to interfere with or destroy them.

There may be little mileage in a return to faith in tree-dwelling fairies, but that sense of the special quality in living plants and animals, and their respect for the power of nature is something worth revisiting.

Parched Earth

The increase in droughts and their severity is one concrete sign of the changing climate. For some regions, falling rainfall means inconvenience. In others, it threatens devastation to people, animals and the whole environment.

In 1996, the American Southwest experienced some of the driest months on record. The fall in wheat harvests led to a shortfall in world stocks. Destructive fires burned out of control on bone-dry land, a problem repeated in Melbourne, Australia, in early 2009.

In Kenya, frequent failure of seasonal rains leads to periods of drought. Pasture land dries up, and without water for crops and livestock, people face painful decisions about whether to abandon their land or undertake backbreaking round trips of many miles to bring back clean drinking water.

Even a small island like Kiribati in the Pacific faces drought. As a coral island, the ground does not hold water reserves. When rainfall is low, people have to rely on tankers to ship in water, and the limited supplies come under extreme pressure.

We may all face drought at some time, and learning water-efficient ways of life is a good way to prepare and make the most of limited supplies.

June 23

How to Power an Island

The beautiful, rugged Isle of Eigg (population 70) in the Scottish Hebrides may seem an unlikely hotbed of green activity. But not being connected to the grid, islanders were all too aware how much coal, kerosene and diesel they were using to heat and light their homes.

Until 2008 that is, when Eigg's own green electricity grid was turned on, providing 95 percent of the island's energy needs, harnessing the renewable power of wind, water and sun.

Since the whole island was purchased by the community in 1997, working to create a sustainable future has been a top priority. They plan to reduce carbon emissions by 70 percent by 2012—a much more ambitious target than any government. Residents and visitors alike will travel around in a community van run on

recycled cooking oil. There will be more recycling, locally produced wood and more experiments in solar power.

Remember: when it comes to embarking on green changes, no man is an island, even if you live on one.

Go With the Grain

Rice is a staple food for half the world's population, and the only major crop that can grow on land submerged in water. Much of the world's rice is grown in Asia by small-scale farmers, but it is also grown in Italy, Brazil, Australia and a number of African countries.

Up to forty different pesticides can be used on conventional rice crops. Food-safety experts have also expressed worry about a strand of rice genetically modified to produce an insecticide. Some biotech firms argue that GM rice could produce much greater yields and tackle global food shortages.

Green campaigners fear that the long-term effects of messing with the genetics of this ancient crop are unknown and argue that smart, sustainable farming is the way to secure food supplies. For example, releasing fish into paddy fields increases the yield from rice and produces a fish harvest from the same land.

So what are we going to do? Rice is still a nutritious and affordable food. Buy organic, shun GM rice and change over to brown rice. Brown rice contains more nutrients than the milled, white version, which also requires more energy to process.

Pesticides are Poison!

You may feel little sympathy for the insects and weeds that get in the way of food production. In conventional farming, it's time to reach for the chemical killers.

But pesticides are indiscriminate. They can be carried by wind and rain to other plants, and any bird or animal rooting around for food can ingest toxins. Many fruits and vegetables on sale are coated in a layer of chemical residue—definitely not recommended for human consumption. Some pesticides are linked to cancers and reproductive problems, others do not break down in the body.

But many question whether they even work in the long term. Bugs and weeds can become resistant to pesticides, so ever more lethal doses are needed to wipe them out. Of the common pests in US agriculture, around 500 insects and 300 weeds are immune to the chemicals designed to kill them.

The time-honored alternative to pesticides—caring for the soil and encouraging predators that eat pests—comes at a far lower cost financially and environmentally. Buy organic food, grown without pesticides (see January 4), and see June 18 for tips on natural pest control.

June 26

Reduce and Recycle Aerosols

The aerosol spray was invented in the 1920s by Norwegian Erik Rotheim, as a better way to wax his skis. Now, the average household sprays its way through 27 aerosols a year, in deodorants, cleaning products and air fresheners, as well as various medical, industrial and agricultural uses.

Aerosols differ from manual spray pumps, as the contents of a pressurized can are propelled out using chemicals. These used to be CFCs (chlorofluorocarbons), but in the 1980s CFCs were blamed for damage to the ozone layer. By 1995, CFCs had largely been phased out of aerosol cans, and the atmosphere was showing some signs of recovery (see September 16 for more).

Yet aerosols should still be treated with caution. They spray chemicals in a fine mist, making it difficult to avoid inhaling them, especially when used indoors. They add to the chemical cocktail in our homes, and we have little knowledge of the effects of prolonged exposure.

Aerosol cans contain tin-plated steel and aluminum and are recyclable. Find out if there is a local collection point, ensure your cans are completely empty and, unlike food and drink cans, do not crush them.

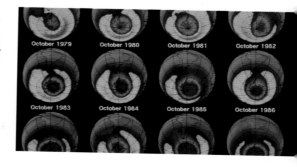

October 1979 · October 1980 · October 1981 · October 1982
October 1983 · October 1984 · October 1985 · October 1986

June 27

Friends Go Free

Spending time with friends needn't be a drain on our resources or the planet's. There are plenty of simple pleasures to be enjoyed, and with warmer, longer days, this is the perfect time of year to discover some of them.

Cycling is a great pace at which to explore a new area—you can cover a lot of ground in a few hours, but it's also easy to stop and admire the view. Or you could take a hike if the weather is fine— why not check out a trail you have never been on before? Or head off to a forest, park, riverside or beach for the day. Leave the car at home and travel on foot, bike or by public transport. Bring kites and a frisbee for entertainment and a hearty home-made picnic.

If you want a little more stimulation, take in a free concert or head for an area where you know there are often street performers or buskers.

Volunteering on a tree-planting or conservation project is a great way to learn a new skill, have a fun day out and achieve something for the local environment.

A Growing Building

A green roof is one that is covered in a layer of soil and vegetation. A grass roof helps blend a rural home with its setting, as well as offering fantastic insulation.

But it is in densely packed cities that green roofs really make their mark. Here, the roof might be used not simply for grass or moss, but to plant small trees, shrubs and even vegetables.

One obvious benefit for city-dwellers is access to greenery, as well as to birds and other wildlife where there are few havens. But a green roof also helps insulate the building from the sun's heat, cold and sound. There is evidence to suggest that a large number of green roofs close together could even help absorb heat, having a cooling effect on the whole neighborhood.

Plants improve air quality by absorbing pollutants. In heavy rainstorms, city drainage systems can be overwhelmed, as a covering of concrete prevents water running off into the ground (see November 30 for better paving options). Green roofs can slow the flow, as water trickles through plants and soil before draining away. To lay the groundwork for a greener world, start at the top!

June 29

Preserving Your Produce

If you are growing your own fruit and vegetables, there are bound to be times when you are overwhelmed by one of your crops. It's worth learning how to preserve them, so you can enjoy the fruits of your labor and have tasty, local produce for much longer. If you have no garden, you can buy in bulk from the farmer's market to see you through the winter.

There are several different processes to choose from, depending on the crop, but most rely on creating conditions in which bacteria and mold can't get down to business.

Freezing is a simple option. Spread the best specimens of mushrooms, berries or tomatoes on a tray so none are touching and freeze. Once they are hard, put them in freezer bags or boxes and they shouldn't stick. Peas and beans can be boiled for a minute or two, then plunged into cold water and frozen.

Acidic foods, including tomatoes and some fruits, can be boiled and then bottled in sterlized jars. Tomatoes from an abundant harvest can also be dried in a food dryer, roasted or made into sauce for freezing or canning.

There are also countless simple and traditional recipes for chutneys, pickles, marmalades and jellies.

Evenings Al Fresco

It's lovely to sit in the yard or on the patio on a summer's evening, but make sure you're not running up your electricity bill in the process.

Patio heaters produce emissions equivalent to those of a speeding truck! Whether gas or electric, they are essentially inefficient because they are there to heat the outdoor air. Put on a sweater instead, or if you can't stand the cold, go back in the kitchen.

If your outdoor walkway needs light, opt for solar-powered ones. These lights have a small solar panel that absorbs sunlight during the day and uses it to light your way at night. Design has come a long way on solar outdoor lights, so they work better than ever. Check out solar-powered string lights and colorful jars with an enchanting glow.

An outdoor gas grill emits half as much carbon and fewer nasty pollutants than a charcoal-fired grill. Or, for the really adventurous, try a solar stove, which emits no carbon at all. Keep your grill clean and covered up between uses so it works efficiently.

July
1

Green Glam

These terms don't always have to conflict. Plastic bags have become the scourge of the green consumer; every minute, over one million bags are used worldwide, but what if these flimsy carriers could become something useful? It is just this desire to reduce waste that has inspired designer Anna Roebuck to start up her own business, Bags2Riches, with the mission to "create desirable objects from everyday waste."

Anna turns donated plastic bags into ornaments, mobiles and fashion bags by fusing the plastic to form new shapes and densities. The company has flourished since 2001, expanding the range to include much thicker and more durable products, including bowls, lampshades and cuff links. Roebuck has become a silversmith in order to create stylish jewelry out of what was once waste.

She also encourages interested parties to send her their old bags: the more colorful the better, so that she can turn them into new, eco-friendly, lasting ones.

To find out more about the Bags2Riches range of unique products and artwork, and how they're made, look at the website.

Bathroom Basics

Disposing of the results of our most basic human function has a significant environmental impact. Every year, each household flushes away thousands of gallons of water, with each flush consuming up to 3 gallons of a precious resource: clean (usually drinking-quality) H_2O.

Graham Hill, founder of the environmental website Treehugger, once famously asked people to save water by following his simple rule: "If it's yellow, let it mellow; if it's brown, flush it down"— but, understandably, this idea just doesn't wash with most people.

A less unpopular solution is the dual-flush toilet, which has two options for how much water is used per flush. Choosing the low-capacity option saves up to 7000 gallons of water in a year. Alternatively, simply replace your toilets with new fittings: today's standard cisterns are smaller than those of older models, saving up to 4000 gallons annually.

If you're ready for a more serious commitment to saving water, the greenest option is to use a compost toilet, which doesn't use water at all (or uses very little), and as an added bonus transforms the waste into useable manure. A high-tech version looks like an ordinary modern WC. Sounds stinky, but a ventilating pipe conducts away the smell.

July 3

LETS Exchange

In a world full of headlines concerning economic crises, it's a relief to find an alternative to spending your savings on increasingly expensive services. Organizations are springing up all over the world to give people the opportunity to swap their time or skills for other services.

Most towns and cities in the UK now have a LETS—Local Exchange Trading Scheme—which gives people the chance to barter. This means they can swap childcare for transport or tool hire for catering through LETS credits, a system of bartering that allows users of the scheme to make cash-free transactions.

U-Exchange is an American-grown bartering website on which members in 82 countries across the world can exchange services such as housesitting, gardening or dog walking. Searching the internet will help you to find something in your area.

There is also the low-tech way to swap skills and services and save the pennies. When it comes to birthdays, holidays or any other kind of celebration, instead of the usual gifts, why not give loved ones a present of your time or services? As belts tighten, such activities can help bring friends and communities together. (See also October 24.)

Organic Meat

The increased availability of organic meat in recent years is a real victory for green consumers. Demand has risen to such an extent that fast-food restaurants have changed their menus, and supermarkets, previously put off by the reduced profit margins, have made concessions to the ethical market by bringing out organic ranges.

Reports on the state of battery-farm chickens, abattoir methods and force feeding have left people looking for ways to ensure the meat they eat is as humanely sourced as possible. With organic farming, the animals lead more natural lives, are not intensively farmed, are fed natural foodstuffs and are not routinely fed drugs. It is also better for the environment, thanks to less disruptive farming methods and fewer chemicals.

This effort to support ethical practices is sweetened by the fact that such meat has been found to be more nutritious, with fewer potentially harmful additives, and GM-free. It is no wonder that people rarely return to mass-produced or processed meat once they have tried organic.

For more information on producers and benefits of organic meat, check out local sites on the internet.

July
5

Hedgerows

Hedges are a traditional element of the British countryside, dividing fields for rotating crops and grazing in old-fashioned farming. But what many people don't realize is that hedgerows are vital to maintaining the ecosystem.

On farms they play an important role in preventing soil erosion, providing shelter, protecting crops from the wind and controlling the movement of livestock, but they are also a crucial habitat for many forms of wildlife. A stinging nettle is a common hedgerow plant and it alone supports 40 different creepy-crawlies.

Without hedgerows many creatures, including birds, reptiles, insects and mammals would struggle for food, protection and a suitable habitat. In spite of this, over recent years, more hedgerows are being removed than are being planted. Volunteers are being sought all over the country to help plant new ones.

If you have a garden of your own, why not plant some typical hedgerow species—hawthorn, dog rose, blackthorn, crabapple trees or blackberries, perhaps? You will be brightening your garden and providing a home for mice, voles, frogs, butterflies and songbirds—inhabitants of the countryside for millennia.

Trash to Treasure

We've all been there: you've cleaned out and sent bags to the recycling, but when there are still some things left that are not in good enough condition to donate or sell on eBay, and you would be embarrassed to give away, what else can you do but throw them out? A novel answer: modern art.

With a little bit of creative flair and imagination, your unwanted items could become garden decorations, a work of art on your patio or even a distinctive sculpture on your front lawn. Chipped or broken plates can be stuck directly into the ground to create pictures or patterns; old mirrors can be attached to fences or trees to bring a magical feel to your garden, which birds and animals will love as much as humans. Old car parts, metal fencing or rusty gates are all suitable materials for the unique piece of artwork that you can create—but take care to clean them up first.

Even old clothes, scarves and umbrellas can be used with a little imagination to turn your balcony or yard into a wonderland to be enjoyed by everyone who sees it. And best of all, getting out into the fresh air to deck out your garden with all your old pieces of rubbish is not only great exercise, it will also help you beat stress.

July
7

Chilling Out

Refrigerators and freezers have long been known as one of the household's biggest culprits when it comes to climate change. Running constantly, these machines can produce thousands of tons of carbon dioxide every year, and account for approximately 17 percent of all domestic energy use.

The good news is that you can keep your milk fresh and your produce frozen while doing less damage to the environment. If possible, all refrigerators and freezers over seven years old should be replaced with a newer model. As with all appliances, make sure you're buying an energy-efficient one and that you dispose of your old one properly. Also, think hard about how big an appliance you really need, as larger models use more energy. Chest freezers are slightly more energy-efficient than upright models.

There are many energy-efficient improvements to newer models. New appliances may have features like alarmed doors to warn you when the door is accidentally left open, and vacation settings so you can save energy when you are not actually using your appliance.

There is no need to use the highest setting, so check your thermometers to make sure yours is appropriate to your needs.

Summer Berries

Summer is the time of plenty for fresh fruits and vegetables, but perhaps nothing is anticipated with as much delight as the arrival of those first juicy berries.

Raspberries, blackberries, blueberries, and almost all other fruits ending in "berry" are ripe and ready for the picking at this time of the year, or soon. If you're lucky enough to live near a source of wild berries, head there first, because wild fruits will often have a more intense flavor, even though they're usually smaller.

Berries are among the worst long-distance travelers of all fruits and veggies. Small, delicate and easily squashed, cultivating a variety that travels well means sacrificing all taste and texture.

Eat fresh berries on their own, with your granola, or in a refreshing fruit salad, or with cream or ice cream. When you've eaten your fill, you could try making them into pies, cobblers or muffins, or using them as a topping for French toast or cakes.

If you have the enviable good fortune of having more berries than you, your family, friends and neighbors can eat, learn how to freeze or preserve them in jams and chutneys for winter.

July 9

Say Cheese!

Digital cameras offer a greener alternative to conventional cameras. They eradicate the need for all those rolls of film and the chemicals used to develop photographs, while dramatically cutting back on the amount of photographic paper used to make prints. So if you're looking to preserve your memories with the minimum impact, go digital.

Keep in mind your impact when sharing your images; while everyone loves to see prints of friends, family or the latest vacation, spare a thought for the environment when you set up your printer, and think carefully about how many pictures you actually need. Just print out your absolute favorites and save the rest on your computer. It is just as easy to show someone a slide show as it is to show them an actual photo album.

If you are a keen outdoor photographer, there are also some rules to consider while out trying to capture that perfect image.

Don't destroy anything in a bid to get your shot; leave things as you find them; take all your trash with you when you go; and don't interfere in any way with animals you might be photographing.

To stay green, photographers should be sure to use rechargeable batteries (see January 8).

The Maori Way

The Maori people of New Zealand see the spirit in every living thing, from animals to trees, from rocks to rainfall. Their belief system is nature-based, and indeed the name *Maori* means pure, or natural. The Maori believe that every aspect of nature—including humankind—is descended from Father Sky and Mother Earth. Even the modern Maori world view is very different to the norm in the West. There is a deep connection to nature. The Maori way is to placate the spirits of the forest before cutting down a tree. One Maori writer describes the adoption of this view as "like putting on a new pair of glasses."

Maori life has always also been greatly dependent on the stars and the skies of the Southern hemisphere, not only for navigation, but for fishing, planting, even making war or choosing peace. The night sky in this culture could be considered as being like a blackboard filled with messages.

While the more scientific approach of Western cultures has given the world many amazing discoveries, it can not explain the spirituality found in nature, and cannot help us when it comes to tuning into our instincts and making wise choices.

July 11

World Population Day

Prompted by the milestone of the world's population reaching five billion (gauged to have been on July 11, 1987), World Population Day, the brainchild of the United Nations Development Program, is held on this day every year as a way of raising awareness of global issues surrounding the Earth's ever-growing population. An increasing population causes problems including habitat destruction, energy use, the disappearance of natural resources and concerns over food security. With the world's population now well on its way to seven billion, these issues are only becoming more urgent.

The United Nations Population Fund (UNFPA) is determined to use World Population Day as a way of working with governments and nongovernment organizations to push for action: to combat HIV, provide family-planning options, promote gender equality, reduce poverty and stabilize population growth as a way of encouraging more prosperous, healthy communities and better living conditions for families all over the planet.

To find out more, see the United Nations website, or look for details of the international Population Clock.

Dog Days

Pet owners who have tried to bathe their dog indoors know just how much of a mess the entire bathroom can be in by the time the family pooch is soaked, scrubbed, dried and ready to curl up in his or her basket for a well-earned nap. Which is why long, hot July days provide the perfect opportunity to wash your pet outdoors—be it in the river or in the garden. Not only does this make the bathing process easier on all involved, it avoids wasting water, an especially limited resource in the summer months; start now, and continue year round!

If you have outdoor space, your family pet will get a good wash in the same water you use on your lawn, flower beds and potted plants. Collect water in butts and use the doggy bathwater on the plants. Follow the same principle when washing your car, instead of visiting the car wash. And if you happen to keep fish, make sure you pour the water from their tanks onto garden plants before refilling with clean; the tank water will be rich in nitrogen and phosphorus, providing a free fertilizer.

Don't overwater your lawn. If your local climate is dry, seed it with drought-loving grasses or opt for a lawn-free yard (see August 8).

July 13

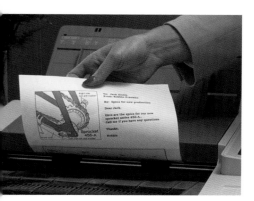

Careful What You Print For

It's as easy as two clicks with the mouse, but is your printing necessary? Ask yourself if the page in question is something that couldn't be jotted down with a pen on the corner of a newspaper or filed electronically instead.

Perhaps you want a hard copy of a map if you are about to set off on a journey, a print of an e-card or a shopping list, or even baking instructions for a birthday cake, but with our planet struggling to cope with the drain humanity places on her resources, it is time to think twice about your paper usage. Four billion trees are cut down every year just to meet our demands for paper.

E-mail is a great way of sending invitations, letters or holiday greetings to friends without using paper, and if you need to save contact details or directions, why not enter the information into your cell phone so you don't use paper at all. In many instances it might even be simpler to keep your internet up and running while you use the information you need.

Think twice before you put pen to paper, and make sure you recycle all the paper you do use. The same sheet of paper can be used by others again and again. And share all your books once you've read them!

Foraging

For thousands of years people survived by living off the land, many as hunter-gatherers, but in recent times we have all but forgotten the natural larder that exists around us. During summertime in particular, nature can provide a veritable feast. Learning how to eat from the wild is fun, too.

Wild strawberries and other berries are all readily available in temperate regions during the summer months, as are leaves, nuts, shoots and roots of many varieties. Wild summer food available near you may include fruits like apples, blackberries, damsons, elderberries, rosehips and sloes, all of which can be transformed into tasty pies, cakes, jams and juices. As well as wild plants, perhaps you can fish in nearby rivers and ponds. If you live in a desert region, you may even be able to find edible cacti.

If you are planning to go picking in your local woods or fields, be very careful to identify accurately anything you find. Mushrooms, berries and leaves may be deadly poisonous, so make sure you know exactly what you are picking.

To find out more, consult a reliable guidebook if you don't know anyone who can show you how to identify what's safe and edible.

Snail Trails

Tropical cone snails are marine gastropod mollusks of the *Conidae* family. They are revered for the beauty of their shells, but less well-known are the amazing medicinal qualities of their venom.

There are up to 500 species of cone snails. The venom, used to immobilize prey, can be fatal to humans in some cases: it's possible to be stung by large cone snails even through a wetsuit. But the venom has a plethora of uses. It yields drugs used to treat pain, cancer and many other serious and chronic conditions, including epilepsy and clinical depression, and researchers are pursuing possible new uses of cone-snail venom to treat Alzheimers.

In spite of this, scientists have warned that cone snails, which mostly inhabit the shallow waters near tropical coral reefs, are in danger of extinction due to habitat destruction, over-exploitation and other human activities. It would be a disaster for humankind to lose the amazing array of pharmaceutical benefits offered by the *Conidae*. Gone, too, would be the great beauty and variety of the cone-shaped shells for which they are named. The use of their beautifully patterned, colorful shells in jewelry may be banned as part of the SOS (save our snails) effort.

Waste Not, Want Not

Every year the average household in the Western world throws away a shocking seven tons of wasted food. In our hectic, stressed lifestyles, it is easy to understand how fruit at the bottom of the bowl gets forgotten, and last night's leftovers end up in the garbage. And while most food biodegrades, it gives off greenhouse gases if not disposed of responsibly. If you do end up with leftovers you can't eat, put them in the compost or a wormery (see February 17 and June 12).

By following just a few simple guidelines, you can dramatically reduce the amount of food you waste.

Food For Thought

- ✔ *Plan your meals and make a shopping list.*
- ✔ *Check what you have in store before you go shopping, so you only buy what you need.*
- ✔ *If you often pick up extras or get tempted by offers to buy "two for ones," give internet shopping a try.*
- ✔ *If you have made too much pasta, stew or soup, freeze leftovers for another meal.*
- ✔ *If your fruit is in danger of turning, try making smoothies before condemning it to the garbage.*
- ✔ *Get creative with leftovers! Not only will using leftovers help reduce food waste, it will save you cash too.*

July 17

Careful Campers

Nothing beats getting out into nature to spend a night under the stars, or under canvas if the weather isn't so good. However, getting back to nature can affect our delicate ecosystem if we are not careful. Here are a few tips for enjoying the great outdoors without having a detrimental effect.

Choosing a site carefully will limit the impact you have on the area. One camping trip might not leave a lasting impression, but a constant stream of campers certainly will. Try to avoid staying in the same spot for more than three nights, because this affects vegetation, and avoid lighting fires if you might cause damage.

Camping in small groups is most fun, but remember that noise can trouble wildlife as well as other humans. Be prepared to move if you realize you are disturbing a nesting site. Make sure you take all scraps of food with you when you leave to avoid attracting unwelcome scavengers; your food isn't good for them anyway.

Wash dishes with bio-degradable solutions only.

Find a toilet site at a safe distance from fresh water.

Don't leave anything behind: even a banana peel will attract animals and disrupt their regular eating habits. Be sure to leave the spot exactly as you found it.

Grow Your Own Sprouts

If you are looking to liven up your garden salad with something homegrown, look no further than sprouts. The good news is that you don't need the greenest of fingers to grow them; sprouts can be grown in your own kitchen. Any edible seed can be sprouted, including mung beans, fenugreek, alfalfa, lentil and radish. Just make sure you buy them from a health-food store to be confident that they haven't been treated with fungicide or other potentially harmful additives, and to make sure they'll germinate.

Once you have your seeds of choice, all you need is a jar, a circle of cheesecloth and a rubber band. Simply place the seeds in the jar, half fill with water, fix the cloth over the mouth of the jar with the rubber band to protect the seeds from light, and then leave to stand for eight to twelve hours. Drain off the water, rinse, and return to the jar; repeat the rinsing twice a day for two days. Sprouts should be ready within four to six days. They will provide a healthy, tasty and, most importantly, homegrown addition to your salad, sandwiches, stir-fries or soups.

July 19

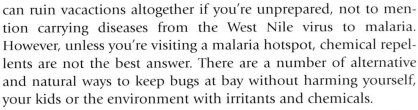

Natural Insect Repellents

Mosquitoes, blackflies, midges and other biting bugs can make summer pretty miserable, and they can ruin vacactions altogether if you're unprepared, not to mention carrying diseases from the West Nile virus to malaria. However, unless you're visiting a malaria hotspot, chemical repellents are not the best answer. There are a number of alternative and natural ways to keep bugs at bay without harming yourself, your kids or the environment with irritants and chemicals.

Taking yeast supplements, garlic tablets or Vitamin B1 for a few days will make your skin secrete a subtle scent to keep the biting beasties away. Citronella, derived from the lemon-scented plant Cymbopogon, also puts off hungry creepy crawlies with its smell. It is available in an array of sprays, creams, candles and sticks. Feverfew is one of several herbs that repel fleas: keep sachets of dried stems in your suitcase or drawers.

Some companies produce repellents made of natural blends of

essential oils that will keep even the most determined insect at arm's length. You can even make your own repellent using olive oil, distilled water and any mixture of citronella oil, or oil of cloves, geranium, cedar, cinnamon, peppermint or lemongrass.

Picnics and Parties

Next time you are planning a picnic or outdoor party, think about what you need to buy, and what you already have at home. You might think you are saving on cleaning up by buying disposable plates, napkins, cutlery and even tablecloths, but when you add it all up, that makes for a lot of waste. There are many ways to reduce your meal's "leftovers."

To start with, if cutlery is short, plan on serving up food that people can eat with their fingers: chicken drumsticks, breadsticks, crudites, quiche slices, mini pies or chips and dips are all firm favorites for parties and picnics. Provide cloth napkins: they stand up to grease far better than a disposable napkin, and they're simple to wash, squeezed in along with a full load of towels. Plastic tablecloths and picnic rugs that can be wiped over are a greener alternative to those you simply throw away.

Drinks always taste better from glasses than paper cups at a house party, while durable plastic "glasses" do fine for the great outdoors. Best of all, after a wash in a bowl of warm, soapy water, or even a cool mountain stream, they are good as new again.

Take Responsibility

In the fast-moving world in which we live, it is easy to fall into the habit of blaming everything from world politics to our bosses for our own unhappiness. As many spiritualists, mystics, New Age gurus and even quantum physicists are beginning to tell us, we are all responsible for our own happiness, and to realize this can be incredibly empowering.

As American life coach Dr Alffie Adagio says: "Often we hand over our personal power to others and then wonder why we become victims. Personal empowerment is when we accept responsibility for our actions and how we live our lives. Others may create problems for us, and maybe Life deals us difficult situations. However, how we handle this is completely up to us." So to help inspire you toward empowerment, here is the Power Prayer, as taken from the famous new-age philosophy *A Course in Miracles*, by Dr Helen Schucman and William Thetford.

Power Prayer

I am responsible for what I see
I choose the feelings I experience
And decide upon the goal
  I would achieve
And everything that seems to
  happen to me...
I ask for, and as I ask, I receive.

Tone It Down

Printer ink cartridges have become an everyday supply for homes and offices. Not only are they expensive, but sending the cartridges to landfill is bad for the environment; they are estimated to take up to 450 years to decompose. In spite of this, something like 85 percent of all ink cartridges bought every year end up in landfill.

There are, however, plenty of things you can do to make sure you get value for money when buying printer ink and to ensure you leave less of an impact on the environment. First of all, many companies supply envelopes or labels for consumers to send old ink cartridges away for recycling. Not only do remanufactured cartridges cost as little as 10 percent of the price of new ones, sending your old cartridges for recycling can benefit a wide range of charities. Best of all, making this change alone can help to reduce the four million litres of oil a year that are consumed by making toner and ink products.

There are also a number of companies that offer a refilling service; this means that all you have to do is send off your empty cartridges and buy a refill, for a much smaller fee than it would cost to buy a new one.

July 23

Pollinator Week

An astounding 75 percent of all plants are pollinated by birds, bees and butterflies. Without them our wonderful planet would lose any number of plants, fruits and vegetables, from maize to apples, squash to almonds.

Honey bees alone pollinate 80 percent of insect-pollinated crops; altogether, more than one-third of the entire world's diet is dependent on such crops. Yet studies show that the number of pollinators, especially bees, is declining through a combination of loss of habitat, viruses and the use of pesticides.

The US Fish & Wildlife Service holds an awareness week each year to help highlight the importance of birds, bees and insects, and the job they perform. The week is also designed to show people what they can do to help.

For example, by choosing garden plants that provide pollen and nectar sources, you can preserve this most natural of production lines. You can also help by providing nest sites for pollinators, such as bee boxes, and by avoiding the use of harmful pesticides. Find out more on the US Fish & Wildlife Service website.

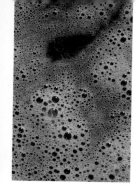

Gray Water

Gray water is nonindustrial waste water, like the water that has been used in dishwashers, washing machines and bathtubs, but does not include toilet waste or waste water from the kitchen sink, which may contain fat and grease. Gallons of the gray stuff can be washed down our drains, but the fact of the matter is that it could all be recycled and used again, for a variety of your everyday water needs around the house and yard.

All you need to be able to do this at home is a Gray Water Diverter Valve. Instead of letting gray water slip away down the drain, a diverter will collect it in a store until it can be reused. Use it to water the garden, wash the car, or to flush the toilet. This small valve will save a whole lot of water, and money.

A word of warning: don't divert water that has bleach products in it. If you are using your washing-machine water on your garden, don't use as much fertilizer, because the water will contain traces of nitrogen and phosphates. It is not advisable to use gray water on your vegetable garden if it contains cleaning products.

Despite these caveats, reusing gray water is a simple, effective way to cut down on your use of precious, clean, drinking-quality water.

July 25

Community Farming

Found in the suburbs of Wollongong in New South Wales, Australia, Dapto is a community with an industrial history. But the town is now embracing sustainability in a big way, with the Dapto Community Farm, a fully organic vegetable farm, at the heart of its efforts.

Participants rent a bed on the farm to grow their own organic produce, for themselves and, if there's any surplus, to sell at a food co-op, organic market or community food sale. Australians have developed a passion for small-scale organic farming!

Dapto's farm project is irrigated carefully to avoid water waste. Groups meet to trade seeds, attend talks and demonstrations and

to share information on everything from poultry rearing to biodynamic planting methods. Their varied program even includes scarecrow workshops, to learn about old-fashioned pest control.

To find out more on community farming, check out the Organic Farming World website. See also April 17 for information on volunteering at organic farms.

Computer Recycling

With the price of computers, especially laptops, dropping all the time, many people are replacing their old computers regularly. Instead of just throwing your old one, and all its accessories you no longer need, into the back of a closet, or even worse, into landfill, there are plenty of opportunities to dispose of them in an environmentally friendly way.

Some manufacturers will collect your old computer, sometimes even a different make, free of charge when you are buying a new one from them. At the time of this writing, Dell is one example.

Chain stores will sometimes take used computers from customers who are buying a similar product: if you're trading in, check that the store will be disposing of it in a green way.

There may be a charity in your area that takes used computers in order to recycle or recondition them. If not, then check out Computer Aid International, a charity specializing in reusing computers in developing countries.

Try freecycling or other donation programs so that someone else can use your computer who might not need (or be able to afford) the latest models on the market.

A word of warning though: make sure that you've safely removed your data before you recycle it.

July 27

Leave 'em Off!

It sounds like such an obvious thing to do, but many people still aren't in the habit of switching lights off when they leave a room. Householders waste anything between 600 and 13,000 watts by leaving lights on around the house while they are out, or simply sitting in other rooms. Businesses and offices have an even greater responsibility when it comes to reducing wasted power with all their excess lighting.

The rules for saving energy are pretty simple. Leave as many lights switched off as possible around your home. Don't switch on all the lights if all you need is one small table lamp. And don't forget to replace all the incandescent light bulbs in your home with energy-saving bulbs (see January 18).

If your company has a policy of leaving lights on overnight, maybe it is time to start petitioning the management to change this wasteful practice. You can stress the amount of money that could be saved by turning off the lights.

If you want to work harder, you could try switching off all the lights for an hour each week. Tell stories, or meditate!

Lavender

The lavender plant provides one of the most useful essential oils around. For thousands of years it has been used to cleanse, soothe and heal wounds, as well as making things smell and taste better. The plant's pale purple leaves make the perfect potpourris and can be sewn into attractive cloth pouches to give a sweet-smelling scent to sock drawers or to keep moths away from clothes hanging in the closet.

Lavender pouches can also be placed under a pillow at night to aid relaxation and a good night's sleep. A few drops of lavender oil on your pillow or in a bath will do just as well. Lavender can also be added to sugar to give it a floral fragrance and taste. The leaves are regularly added to blends of black, green and herbal tea for their scent, flavor and calming properties.

Chefs in Provence have long added the plant to their culinary creations. The oil can even be added to witch hazel as an anti-inflammatory for insect bites and burns. Lavender plants are wonderful growing in your garden for the fragrance alone.

As with all herbal remedies, you should consult a doctor before using lavender therapeutically, especially if you're pregnant.

July 29

Paint Your Home Green

Many household paints are full of potentially dangerous substances. If you're redecorating with regular paint, the air inside your house could be polluted with volatile organic compounds, including benzene and formaldehyde, or even lead, if the paint is old. Paint solvents are dangerous to people with heart conditions and can aggravate asthma.

In recent years there has been a move to produce paints that are less harmful to people—and to the environment. Traditional substances like limestone, clay and even milk can be used in paints. Limestone in particular is a great alternative: it can be tinted various colors and allows the surface being painted to "breathe," preventing the build-up of damp and resultant damage to walls.

Research your paint before you start decorating. When you're done, old or unused paint can be recycled, but it has to be done carefully. Don't just pour it down the drain; check where you can safely recycle it in your area. Better still, you could pass on all your unused paint on to someone else who has a use for it.

Just a Walk in the Park

More than 12 percent of the world's land is protected in parks and reserves. Yet many national park areas are greatly underused. Despite having many miles of forested walkways, marked trails, campsites and wildlife-spotting activities, the vast majority of park visitors only walk the distance from their car to the visitor center, shop or café.

So, now is the time to make the most of our planet's wonderful natural spaces. Everyone knows that fresh air and exercise are good for the body, but getting out and about to experience the natural world is also good for the spirit. Walking in a natural setting can have similar effects to meditation, helping to reduce stress, but with the added bonus of promoting physical fitness.

Open parklands are also the perfect places to take the family for an active day out, where plenty of good old-fashioned fun can be had with a ball, frisbee or simply cooling off in a stream or pond. Best of all, our beautiful parklands, forests, woodlands and reserves are, generally, either free or else accessed for only a nominal fee.

As with any outdoor activity, remember to not disturb animals or leave any waste behind. Don't spoil others' enjoyment by playing loud music if you're in a tranquil spot.

July 31

Own Your Store

A food co-op is a nonprofit organization formed by a group of people who want good quality, healthy food at affordable prices. A food co-op may be run more like a club than a formal co-operative. Most are owned by their customers, staff, or some combination of these.

Founded in 1973, the Park Slope Food Co-op in Brooklyn, New York, is a successful and popular organization that requires its members to contribute their labor in return for the benefits of shopping for healthy food and sharing in the ownership. Prices are kept down by the lack of labor costs, and committees meet to make major decisions. Like most co-ops, there's an emphasis on ethically sourced and local, organic food.

There are many specialist food co-ops, for example, for vegans and vegetarians. Being part of a co-op brings great benefits. You have more control of how your food is produced. You can buy healthy, local food at a lower price and with a clean conscience. You'll meet like-minded people, and you can spend your money ethically.

That beautiful season the Summer!
Filled was the air with a dreamy and magical light;
  and the landscape
Lay as if new created in all the freshness of childhood.
    —Henry Wadsworth Longfellow

August
1

Buying Vintage Clothes

Looking for a change from the homogeneity of chain stores? Why not try going vintage?

By wearing a classic Chanel suit, an original Mary Quant mini skirt or a Dior evening gown from the 1930s to a party, you can guarantee that no one else is going to be wearing the same thing. Donating to, and shopping at, second-hand stores is the best way for the stylish shopper to reduce their waste and save money.

As fans of vintage clothing have discovered, many garments made by classic designers, especially those made before 1980, have a better cut, superior stitching and a better quality of fabric than anything you could buy today for the same money. Overall, there are fewer worries about production quality: these are clothes that have stood up to the test of time.

At second-hand clothes stores you can pick up anything from designer classics to old favorites like skinny jeans. As shoppers become more frugal and the environmental impact of the fashion industry becomes more evident, vintage fairs are becoming ever more popular. It's a great change from the same old looks that fill the major chain-store windows.

Remember the Elephants

The Amboseli Elephant Trust in Kenya is the longest-running study of wild elephants in the world, and one of the most celebrated. Everyone at the trust works hard to benefit the wellbeing of these mighty creatures, as well as their habitat and their human fans.

Ever since Cynthia Moss first started observing the elephants of the Amboseli ecosystem, which feeds off the waters of Mount Kilimanjaro, in 1972, the elephants have become a source of fascination. The revelations learned from Amboseli form the basis of contemporary understanding of elephants and provide the knowledge needed to protect them and their habitat.

The trust provides outreach support to the local Maasai communities by providing secondary education bursaries and university scholarships in the hopes that the promising youngsters will one day return to the area with their newly acquired skills. They also provide "consolation" payments to any local herders who have lost livestock to elephants.

The Amboseli Elephant Trust website provides plenty more information.

August 3

Man's Best Friend

As the dog days of summer begin, it's important to remember that not just farm animals but also domestic pets need to be treated humanely.

Sadly, this is not the case for many pets sold commercially. Far too many puppies sold are bred in "puppy mills." Young pups, many not even old enough to be weaned, are kept in overcrowded, unhealthy conditions, much like battery chickens (unfortunately, the puppies are often kept in chicken cages, without room to move). In addition to physical risks, such dogs are often poorly socialized and do not make good pets; as a result they do not find homes and are put down. As a result, the life of a "puppy mill" dog will likely be short and miserable. "Kitty mills" also exist to exploit that other popular pet choice.

By buying only from reputable breeders who are transparent about the conditions in which they raise animals, we can put a stop to such heartbreaking practices. Adopting a shelter animal is even better. After all, a purebred won't love you any more than that adorable little mutt with the lopsided ears.

Parents for Air Quality

Every parent wants the best for their child and the most basic way to ensure a child's wellbeing is to make sure that the air they breathe is as pure as possible.

The air outside can be filled with pollution caused by traffic, energy use and factory emissions; even indoors, mold spores, chemical fumes and cigarette smoke can mean the air our children breathe is far from pure. Harm from such pollution can manifest itself in itchy eyes, sore throats, nausea and headaches.

Recently, parents in London were so concerned about air pollution that they campaigned against the relocation of their children's school; the move offered better facilities but in a more polluted area. Parents concerned about air quality can, first of all, speak to their child's school principal to ensure that the school is doing everything possible to make certain that the air the children breathe in school is clean.

Parents or anyone else concerned about the quality of air indoors and outdoors in their area can check out cleanair.com for advice and further information.

August 5

Clean Up Your Environment

Discarded waste is a problem across the globe, with the estimated 4.5 trillion cigarette butts dropped worldwide being a particular problem. Like many other common items of litter dropped, such as plastic bags, fast-food cartons and drink cans, cigarette butts can take years to fully biodegrade, while also posing a threat to wildlife.

Quite why people litter is anybody's guess, although many people believe it is a simple case of laziness, coupled with a lack of pride in community. The good news is that there is a simple and effective method of solving the litter problem. All you need to do is encourage friends and neighbors to get together every so often for a neighborhood clean-up.

It is amazing the difference an hour of hard work can make. Many hands can make light work of improving the environment. You could even turn a litter collection into a monthly event, with people taking it in turns to supply drinks and cookies for the volunteers.

Cafés and Coffee Tips

Whether your preference is a chain store with its supersized sofas or a local corner café, café culture is now a big part of our everyday lives and coffee is one of our biggest guilty pleasures. So what can we do about the environmental effect of such a large industry? There are ways that to ensure that your daily caffeine dose does not have a detrimental effect on the earth and her people. Here are a few tips:

❀ Avoid styrofoam cups at all costs—this plastic is very unfriendly to the environment as it takes many years to biodegrade.

❀ Look for shade coffee: made from beans grown under the natural tree canopy, eradicating the need for tree clearance.

❀ You don't need to find "eco" cafés in order to drink environmentally friendly coffee. Most good cafés and coffee houses sell green and fairtrade coffee if you just take the time to look.

❀ Look for out for the ECO-OK labels, a certifying program run by the non-profit New York group Rainforest Alliance. ECO-OK approved plantations must grow coffee in shade forests, and manage production in an environmentally sensitive manner.

❀ Coffee certified as "bird-friendly" means you can be assured that it is also shade-grown and organic.

August 11

Geology Rocks!

Rocks are the foundation of the earth, yet many of us don't fully appreciate the beauty that lies beneath our feet. To spread some love for our planet's geology, here are a few of the world's best rocks.

Uluru: formerly known as Ayers Rock, this large lump of sandstone dominates the skyline for miles around in the Northern Territory, central Australia. Sacred to the Aboriginal people of the area, this amazing natural form is also a World Heritage Site.

Cappadocia: an area of Turkey dominated by rock phenomena known as "fairy chimneys," caps of hard rock resting on cone-shaped pinnacles of softer rock, making them popular tourist attractions. Some have even been turned into houses.

Amah Rock: this naturally occurring rock is found on a hilltop

in southwest Sha Tin in Hong Kong. Approximately 49 feet in height, it looks like a baby carrying a baby on her back.

Petra: not a natural phenomenon, but a true testament to the beauty of rock. This World Heritage Site (left) is renowned for its rock-cut architecture, although its origins are still uncertain.

Dive Right In!

Swimming in a chlorine-filled pool is one way to get some exercise and gain some water experience, but it never comes close to the experience of jumping with wild abandon into the sea or a river pool. Showering under an icy waterfall is also another must-experience sensation. However, there are a few things to bear in mind before you head for the beach or your nearest secluded lake.

Build up your strength in a swimming pool, and it is a good idea to do some other aerobic exercise to improve your general fitness before attempting anything too ambitious in the sea.

Have a positive attitude, but don't overstretch yourself.

If you have the type of body that sinks more quickly than others in fresh water, you'll probably find it easier to swim in the sea.

Swimming long distances can be quite a meditative exercise, allowing you to focus on stroke tempo and giving you time to think without the interruption of the phone, email or children.

Be aware of tides and currents, and if you are planning on swimming in cold water, wear a swim suit and cap and have a large towel and a thermos of hot tea waiting for you back on land.

August
13

Florence Brown Project

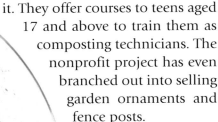

The Florence Brown Community School is a school in Bristol, England, for children with special needs and claims that it is "a school without walls." One of the school's projects is Community Composting, designed to process the green waste of the school and local community.

In the beginning, it was a modest operation in which the schoolchildren gathered together the privet-hedge cuttings, grass clippings and conifer branches to mulch them in a small shredder, but it wasn't long before a much bigger operation was needed, thanks to its popularity among locals. The project also started helping elderly people to reclaim overgrown gardens.

With the help of grants, the school was able to buy an ECO green composting machine with a grab crane and weighing machine and a small tractor to tow and power it. They offer courses to teens aged 17 and above to train them as composting technicians. The nonprofit project has even branched out into selling garden ornaments and fence posts.

To find out more, take a look at the school's website.

August 14

Recycling Scrap Metal

Recyclable metals can be found in any number of everyday objects, including computers, cars, packaging and buildings designated for renovation or demolition.

Every year, 24 tons of aluminum and 1.05 billion tons of steel are produced; this accounts for around 8 percent of the waste sent to landfill by the average household. This is needless, because most metals can be recycled indefinitely.

Recycling aluminum requires just 5 percent of the energy required by primary production and produces only 5 percent of the CO_2 emissions, making it the most cost-effective of all metals to recycle. Sending just one aluminum can to the recycling saves enough energy to run a television for three hours.

Steel cans are also fully recyclable: that includes cans such as deodorant, hairspray and paint cans. Every ton of steel packaging recycled saves 1.5 tons of iron ore, 0.5 tons of coal, 40 percent of the water required in production and 75 percent of the energy needed to make virgin steel.

Check out your nearest recycling depot to find out more, or take all your scrap metal to your local scrap merchant.

August
15

Calling Costs

Cell phones have become the fastest-spreading gadget phenomenon of recent years, with around 980 million sold every year around the world. In spite of this, many people don't realize what an utterly destructive impact such popularity has on the environment.

Cell-phone networks use around 61 billion KWh of energy worldwide, and every one of the millions of base stations across the globe produces 10 tons of carbon emissions every year. Conservative estimates reckon this will double by 2011. The good news is that many of the world's biggest cell phone companies are making efforts to improve their green rating.

One way you can reduce the impact of your phone usage is to make sure to dispose of it safely. Covers and key pads contain chromium and brominated flame retardants; LCD screens contain liquid crystals; circuit boards include lead; and batteries are made from cadmium, nickel and lithium.

Another way to lessen the impact of your cell phone usage on the environment is to make sure that you unplug your phone charger as soon as your phone is charged—otherwise it continues to consume energy.

August 16

Simple Living

In an age of extreme consumerism, it makes a refreshing change to once more start enjoying some of life's simple pleasures. One way to do that is to have a wholesome meal. To do so doesn't mean you have to go out to a fancy restaurant: having a home-cooked meal with your partner, family or friends can actually be even more fun.

Nor does your meal have to be a cordon bleu experience. Sometimes the best meals are those made from simple, local, seasonal ingredients. In summer, that could include a fresh salad with warm chicken and freshly baked bread or cold pasta salad made with fresh plum tomatoes, red onions and mushrooms.

To make the most of your meal, make sure the TV is turned off so that those eating don't have any distraction from their food or conversation. Even if your dinner doesn't mark any particular occasion, make the meal itself an occasion; dress the table with a fresh tablecloth, wild flowers and a jug of iced water. Why not make the most of the hot summer evenings and eat outside? Just remember those special candles to keep away the bugs!

August 17

GM Foods

There has been a much discussion in recent years about genetically modified (GM) food. While some people see its research into our use of the genes as a great opportunity for the future, others reckon that gene research interferes with the natural order. To help you understand the GM debate better, here are some of the basic arguments for and against:

Proponents say:

✔ GM foods have better resistance to weeds, pests and disease.

✔ They have a better texture and flavor, a longer shelf life, a better yield, use fewer herbicides and other chemicals.

✔ There are many safeguards in place.

✔ Changing a gene or two here or there does not make foodstuffs unacceptable.

✔ Necessary if we are to feed the world.

Opponents say:

✗ It is unnatural, or our scientists are "playing God."

✗ Do we really know what we are doing and what the risks are?

✗ Do we really need genetically modified food?

✗ There are better ways to improve resistance and reduce the use of chemicals on the land.

Pandas

Giant pandas have long been the face of animal conservation, and there is no animal better suited to the task. With its gentle baby face, black eyes and cuddly, teddy-bearlike body, this iconic bear provides just the encouragement we humans need to take better care of the world in which we live, and particularly of the animals with whom we share it.

Such is the widespread popularity of the panda that it is easy to forget that these animals are on the cusp of extinction. Recent reports suggest that there are only around 1590 of the bears living in the wild, with a further 239 living in captivity in China and another 27 in zoos around the world. Although other reports suggest that, thanks to recent conservation efforts, panda numbers might be on the rise, there is still not enough proof to take the animals off the endangered list.

In recent years the panda has also become an important symbol of China, second only to the dragon. It is often depicted on coins, reclining in relaxation while chewing on a bamboo shoot. However, that image of relaxation is only an image; pandas still have a long way to go before their future is truly that secure.

August 19

Can't Eat Just One?

Everyone loves to snack on potato chips, but instead of eating store-bought ones that are, more often than not, filled with additives, unhealthy fats and who-knows-what other chemicals, why not try making your own? Just as tasty as those you buy from the store, they are also far and away healthier for you.

You don't need to stick to making chips from potato, either: chips from beetroot, carrot and parsnip are just as delicious. All you really have to do is thinly slice a potato, or whatever other vegetable you feel like trying, and deep fry the slices.

For healthier chips, make sure your oil is vegetable and ensure that it is very hot and that there is plenty of room for each chip to turn unhindered. If you want to make your potato chips particu-

larly healthy keep the skins on when you fry them, as these contain vitamins. Then all you have to do is dry the chips off on paper towel (use sparingly!) and then add whatever seasoning or flavoring you like, from salt to paprika, if any at all. **Warning**: hot oil can easily catch fire!

Dry Not-So-Clean

We all have delicate clothing or household furnishings that need to be dry cleaned, yet doing so is not good for the environment, as the process uses a toxic substance known as PERC. There are, however, now such things as organic dry-cleaning companies, who get stubborn stains out of clothes and curtains with a greatly reduced impact on our planet. Check out the internet to find one in your local area.

Be warned, though, that some dry cleaners might advertise themselves as organic when they are not strictly so. Before you hand over your delicate items for a wash, ask the dry cleaner if they are using the carbon-dioxide cleaning process. During this process CO_2 gas is put under high pressure to convert it into a liquid. As a liquid it acts as a carrier of biodegradable soaps; once the cycle is complete, the majority of it turns back into gas.

Some so-called organic dry cleaners actually use a hydrocarbon solvent called DF-2000. While not as toxic as the process used by ordinary dry cleaners, it is petroleum based, which means it contributes to global warming.

August 21

New-found Species

Changes in the environment have meant that while some forms of life are under threat of extinction, others are only just being discovered. Here is a list of some of the most intriguing new discoveries of recent times:

❀ Central Ranges Taipan: one of the most venomous snakes in the world, the Central Ranges Taipan was discovered in Australia in 2007. Its discovery will help scientists to create more effective snakebite treatments.

❀ Mindoro stripe-faced fruit bat: with large eyes and striped face, this large bat is only found on the Philippine island of Mindoro. The discovery is advancing research on endemic species.

❀ Malo Kingi jellyfish: this lethal species was discovered when it killed American tourist Robert King in Australia in 2002. The jellyfish was later named after its tourist victim.

❀ Clouded Leopard: hailed as a modern-day saber-tooth, thanks to its long fangs. This fearsome creature was found deep in the Borneo rainforests. It can kill its prey, including monkeys, deer and pigs, with a single bite.

Leaks

There is little point in fitting out your home with great insulation, switching to energy-saving light bulbs and using your old shower water to water the garden if you have leaky pipes. What might seem like a small drip could in fact be wasting gallons of water every year. Water coming through roofs and windows can cause a whole range of problems, too.

Fixing leaking pipes will not only save water, but if it is a case of water coming in from the outside it will also save cash, energy, and help prevent mold and mildew from getting established in the home. Mold and mildew can lead to rot, structural damage, paint flaking, and a myriad of health problems, as inhaling or touching mold spores can cause allergic reactions as well as triggering asthma attacks.

In general, if water is leaking through your window, it has not been installed properly. Leaks around the bathtub are caused by missing tiles or cracks in the shower. If the leaks occur around the toilet bowl, they could be caused by broken pipe fittings, a cracked bowl, or the deterioration of the seal around the base of the bowl.

To find more useful hints, check out AsktheBuilder.com.

August 23

Back to School

Returning to school can be an exciting, if stressful, time for both children and parents, but there are ways to take the pressure off while also making the start of a new school year kinder to the environment as well. Here are ways to get the family ready for the return.

❀ Ease the family back into early-morning routines by gradually returning to early mornings and early nights for the last two weeks of summer vacation.

❀ Make packed lunches the night before, remembering to use as little packaging as possible. Plastic containers that can be washed every night work perfectly.

❀ Get your little ones used to the idea of a walk or cycle to school before the summer ends, if you live in a city. Do a couple of practice runs in the week before school starts to see how long it takes and to get the children used to the trip.

❀ Think carefully about what your child really needs in terms of new school clothes. Don't buy a whole new wardrobe if last year's clothes are still the right size and not worn out.

Cosmetic Differences

Thinking about an environmentally friendly way to use toiletries could go a long way to helping to reduce your carbon footprint. For example, do we really need to buy shower gel when a much longer-lasting bar of soap would do?

Do women have to have a different moisturizer for every part of their body when they could use more natural alternatives? Why not try olive oil in the bath instead of body lotion, and home-made body scrub, made from sea salt and olive oil, rather than buying an exfoliating scrub? One simple moisturizer would surely do for everything else.

Try to buy refills where you can; not only are these cheaper, they also need less packaging. Go for pump-action sprays rather than aerosols, and when you have finished with a bottle, rinse it out and make sure it is recycled. Or you could keep the bottle and refill it later with your own homemade beauty products. Just about every-thing from face masks to shampoos can be made from some of the most basic, inex-pensive ingredients stored in your kitchen.

For more homemade, natural beauty suggestions, see January 9.

August 25

Owls

These striking-looking birds of prey have always captured the imagination. Artists love to paint them, poets write about them and many children's stories, including Winnie the Pooh, have a wise, old owl character. However, while the bird's large, staring eyes may well give the impression of intelligence and wisdom, there is no evidence to suggest that they are actually any more intelligent than any other bird of prey.

What they certainly are, though, is striking, with plumage that can range from the purest white of the snowy owl to the mottled browns of a tawny owl. Some owls even have piercing orange eyes and, of course, they are also known for being able to turn their heads a full 360 degrees.

Normally solitary and nocturnal creatures, they feed on small mammals, insects and other birds and, in some instances, fish. They live on every continent on earth except for Antarctica and most of Greenland. Interestingly, the collective noun for a group of owls is a parliament.

August 26

Rag and Bone

Gone are the days of the old-time British "rag and bone men," who went round street by street collecting unwanted items, including rags to make paper from, bones to make glue from and scrap iron to be melted down and used again, swapping goods for trinkets. Their time has passed, but we should all be trying to emulate the rag and bone man's recycling ethos. Think how much better we all would be if, instead of sending our junk to landfill, we found some other purpose for it.

Wouldn't it be better to reuse, recycle or simply finish off something that someone else is done with, rather than buying new things? Your neighbor might have a spare can of paint you could use, while you might be about to throw away a book he has always been desperate to read. He might even be endlessly grateful for your leftover dinner for his own supper.

Explore your area to find out what bartering or swap groups are out there already, and if you don't have any luck finding one, why not set up your own? Websites such as eBay or Freecycle might also help you trade in things you don't want for things you do, or else convert unwanted items into cash.

August 27

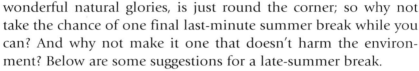

Days of Summer

It is the end of August and the long summer days are slowly coming to an end. Fall, with all its wonderful natural glories, is just round the corner; so why not take the chance of one final last-minute summer break while you can? And why not make it one that doesn't harm the environment? Below are some suggestions for a late-summer break.

❀ Take a cycling vacation: the greenest form of transport is also the perfect way to see the scenery, while getting healthy.

❀ Camping: campers need to abide by a few rules to make sure they are not impacting on the environment, but camping is a cheap, fun activity suitable for all the family. It is a great way to immerse yourself in nature and discover new places, too.

❀ Walking: another great way to get fit, enjoy nature and get to know somewhere new without doing any harm to the ecosystem.

❀ Volunteering: there are any number of ways you can combine your vacation with volunteer work. Check out the charity guide on the net.

Pack a Mat

Bonnie Stromme, an inventive mother of four from Colorado, found herself caught short when she needed to wrap six sandwiches but only had three sandwich bags left. She didn't realize at the time that by improvising with paper towel and masking tape, she was making the first prototype of her green invention. Her Wrap-n-Mat is a reusable sandwich bag that also acts as a placemat, whether in school dining halls, on picnic tables or elsewhere. It is also easy to wash.

No longer do people need to go through dozens of sandwich bags each week; just take a look at the Wrap-n-Mat website for more details. Another enterprising woman has made a business out of making mats and rugs out of plastic bags: perfect for front steps, on boats, on picnic tables, or in the dog basket. No two mats are ever the same, as the print, color and design of the plastic bags used to make them are preserved.

August 29

Planning Ahead

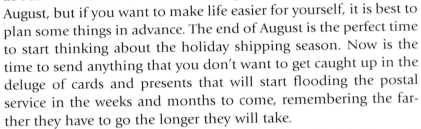

There are not many people who like to think about Christmas and the holiday season in August, but if you want to make life easier for yourself, it is best to plan some things in advance. The end of August is the perfect time to start thinking about the holiday shipping season. Now is the time to send anything that you don't want to get caught up in the deluge of cards and presents that will start flooding the postal service in the weeks and months to come, remembering the farther they have to go the longer they will take.

It is advisable to check out last mailing dates for Christmas at this time as well. You might have up to the end of November or the start of December to send a card to your friends and relatives in distant lands, but it is better to get those cards mailed sooner

rather than later to ensure that they get there on time. You can also send by surface mail rather than air, if you're early enough.

Another good reason to think about doing your holiday shopping now is to make sure any presents you want to order get delivered in plenty of time. If an order does get lost, you've got lots of time to track it down.

Healthy Suspicions

Labor-saving devices always look like a great idea.

How wonderful is it to have a cup of coffee ready for you at your bedside when you wake up in the morning? Or isn't it great that you can now buy a machine that will chop, slice and dice your vegetables any which way you want them? And yes, many of them really do make our lives easier. Can you imagine life without a washing machine, vacuum cleaner or modern oven? It is hard. (See March 16 for Fiona Houston's experiment in life without electricity.) But what you have to bear in mind is that labor-saving often means using energy needlessly.

So, most of us will agree that it is no longer practical to wash all the family's clothes by hand. But do we really need a machine to chop vegetables when we could do the same job in just a few minutes using nothing more than a sharp knife? And let's be honest, how many people do you know who own blenders, breadmakers or ice-cream makers who actually get much use from them?

Chopping the veggies will always take time and energy; the only question is whether it will be yours or the planet's.

August 31

Precious Water

Water might be the Earth's greatest natural resource, but the truth of the matter is that it takes energy and money to make sure that water is clean enough to drink. In some parts of the world clean drinking water is so expensive that poor families must make huge sacrifices in order to make sure that they have safe water, one of life's most basic necessities.

Environmentalists often suggest digging solar stills to collect fresh, uncontaminated water, but in truth it just isn't practical. Figures suggest that there are around one billion people around the world who don't have access to clean water. The UN climate panel estimates that up to 250 million people in Africa will face "water stress" by 2020, causing yields from rain-fed farming in some areas to fall by up to 50 percent.

A new desalination plant has recently been opened in Algiers with the intention of providing the three million people who live there with sea water fit for drinking. The big problem is that healthy water is not free, so to find out more about how you can help take a look at Water Aid International's website.

Oh! how I love, on a fair summer's eve,
When streams of light pour down the golden west,
And on the balmy zephyrs tranquil rest
The silver clouds, — far, far away to leave
All meaner thoughts, and take a sweet reprieve
From little cares; to find, with easy quest,
A fragrant wild, with Nature's beauty drest,
And there into delight my soul deceive.
There warm my breast with patriotic lore,
Musing on Milton's fate — on Sydney's bier —
Till their stern forms before my mind arise:
Perhaps on wing of Poesy upsoar,
Full often dropping a delicious tear,
When some melodious sorrow spells mine eyes.

—John Keats

September
1

The White Stuff

The start of September sees the UK celebrate organic fortnight. Now is the perfect time for you to introduce organic produce into your everyday life, if you haven't yet made a start. Changing your milk is one of the easiest ways to improve your green credentials in the kitchen.

Here, we take a look at some of the reasons why it makes good sense to opt for organic milk:

❋ **Health**: Research has found that organic milk does not contain as many additives or come into contact with as many chemical pesticides. Organic milk does contain more Vitamin A, Vitamin E and antioxidants than regular milk.

❋ **Environment**: Organic farming encourages natural wildlife, helping to maintain rich, naturally balanced soil. By using natural

farming methods, organic farmers ensure that nitrates are released into the environment gradually and not in excess.

❋ **Animal welfare**: The aim of organic farmers is to have happy, healthy cows; they do not force-feed or use drugs to boost their milk production. Cows are kept outside in natural sunlight as much as possible.

Let Us Prey

Birds of prey are among the most visually striking creatures on Earth. Spectacular plumage, fierce eyes, and impressive aerial acrobatics make them some of the most fascinating of all birds, so it's little wonder that so much effort has been put into saving many species from extinction.

One of the most serious threats to endangered birds is pesticides; although now banned, DDT poisoned a principal food source—fish—and even those birds who survived often had eggs that were so fragile that the shells collapsed before the chick could be born, and the birth rate for many species plummeted.

In America, the bald American eagle, the national symbol, was on the brink of extinction when the Endangered Animals Act was introduced in 1967; however, thanks to conservation projects, by 1994 the bird was taken off the endangered list in most US states.

The California Condor is also undergoing a gradual but steady increase. In 1987, the species was almost extinct; the surviving 22 birds were all captured, and a breeding program began. Through a program of captive breeding and release, the number has now climbed to over 300 birds, and continues to rise.

September 3

Writing Right

Disposable pens might seem to be a handy convenience, but the truth is that throwaway plastic ballpoint pens are a hazard for the environment. Consider for a moment the thousands of pens that we each must have gone through in our lifetimes, especially as they are cheap and easily lost.

In 2005, Bic announced the sale of its 100 billionth disposable pen; if they were all laid end to end, they would circle the Earth 348 times. All those pens, whether lost or thrown away, inevitably end up in landfills or waterways.

However, the only real alternative to using disposable pens is to use a refillable pen and good old-fashioned ink. They may cost a little bit more—and it does mean being more careful not to lose them—but making this change will help save the planet from the impact of all that plastic.

There has yet to be a major initiative to recycle these disposable pens. There is one alternative though: send them to The Pen Guy, and he will use them for works of art. Check him out at: pen-guy.blogspot.com

September 4

Heritage Seeds

Gardeners across the world often swap leftover seeds to enhance the variety and heritage of the plants in their own gardens. This is a vital way of conserving rare and sometimes less popular seed varieties, as well as some heirloom species. Buying heirloom varieties is also a good way to avoid inadvertently introducing genetically modified plants.

There are many online organizations, clubs and societies that arrange seed swaps between members; one of the largest is the UK's Garden Organic's Heritage Seed Library. It is designed to make rare varieties of vegetable seeds available to keen gardeners. At least 50 percent of the seeds are provided by the library's "seed guardians": volunteers who grow many of the seeds for the 40,000 packets the library sends out each year.

The library sends out an annual catalogue of the 200 seed varieties they have on offer. For more information, or to find out how to become a member , take a look at the Garden Organics website www.gardenorganic.org.uk. A similar organization is the Seed Saver's Exchange www.seedsavers.org.

September 5

New Life for Old Plastic

Hundreds of millions of plastic bottles are now recycled every year, but have you ever wondered just what can be done with your old water bottle, shampoo bottle or soap dispenser? Recycled plastics can be used in a surprisingly wide range of products, from toys and shoes to electrical equipment and cars. As plastics make up around 7 percent of all household waste, recycling your plastics helps to greatly reduce landfill.

You could try cutting up plastic bottles to make "sleeves" to protect your seedlings in the garden. And see the panel for some of the many products that are made from recycled plastics.

Check out your local recycling options and make sure to only recycle accepted plastics.

Recycled Plastics

- PVC garbage bags
- Shopping bags
- Plastic sewage pipes
- Window frames
- CD and DVD cases
- Outdoor furniture
- Sleeping bags
- Fleece fabrics
- Fencing
- Office accessories

274

Recipes for Efficiency

Everyone enjoys a home-cooked meal, which is sure to be greener than a prepared, processed one, but cooking still consumes plenty of household energy. The average family cooks 1½ meals a day, with each meal taking at least 30 minutes of cooking time to prepare. Energy-efficient cooking is one of the easiest ways to cut your household fuel bills.

When you cook, make sure you use as small a pan and as little water as possible. Using lidded pots and pans helps.

If you do have something cooking in the oven, resist the urge to peek, as this lets out heat, meaning that more energy is needed to raise the temperature again.

When doing stove-top cooking, use a pressure cooker, as these need less time to cook, and hence less energy. Also, if you have a gas stove, make sure the flame is burning blue; a yellow flame indicates that your hob is not using the fuel efficiently.

Reduce cooking time by defrosting foods first and make sure that air can circulate freely around the food, as this helps it cook more quickly.

Go Green, Blue, Red...

In this modern, synthetic age it is easy to forget just what an abundance of gifts Mother Nature provides. Natural dyes bring color to materials without harming the environment. Roots, flowers and plants can all be used to make dyes in a range of colors, from orange to blue.

Here's a quick guide to making your own dye.

When you gather natural materials for dyes, make sure that the blossoms are in full bloom, berries are ripe and nuts mature (and remember never to gather more than two or three plants of the same species). Then chop the plant material into small pieces and add double the volume of water to plant material. Bring them to the boil and simmer for an hour.

Steep your fabric in the dye, simmering for a while, leaving it in the cold water overnight for a deeper shade, making sure the fabric has been soaked in a dye fixer first: salt for berries and vinegar for plant dyes.

For orange, turmeric, onion skin and bloodroot are good options; teabags, oak bark and walnut give shades of brown; use raspberries, rose and lavender for pinks; red cabbage and blackberry for blue; and use beetroot, dandelion roots and hibiscus flowers for reds.

September
8

Simple Pleasures

Ever thought about starting a vegetable patch in your garden, or perhaps growing your own herbs? Becoming more self-sufficient is one of the best ways to limit the impact we have on the environment, while also helping us cut down on bills without giving up any of our favorite fresh foods.

A great deal of satisfaction and pleasure can be found in learning new skills that help you to lead a more environmentally friendly life. Gathering berries to make jams, foraging for nuts and mushrooms, and baking your own bread are all fun ways to limit your carbon footprint. Making your own tea infusions, homemade toiletries and sewing can all be satisfying hobbies that also help the environment. Best of all, having a skill such as jam making means that you are never stuck for ideas when you need to give someone a present.

Making your own is good for your health, as well as the planet's. When you make your own food, you avoid the unnecessary preservatives, salt and sugar that are often added to prolong shelf life; these add nothing to the taste or nutritional value of the food we eat.

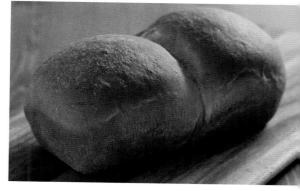

September 9

Suds Sense

Most people are guilty of using far too much water when they wash the dishes. The urge for nice, clean dishes quite often overrides our green sensibilities as we fill sink after sink with steaming hot water and leave the cold water running in order to rinse them well. In reality, all we need to do our dishes is one small basin of warm, soapy water for washing and another small basin half filled with cold water for rinsing. Buy a tub to fit inside your basin if you have a large kitchen sink.

When you have finished with the water, instead of simply letting it go down the drain, think whether there is anything else that the water could be used for, such as washing the kitchen floor, washing the car or even flushing the toilet.

Another tip to remember when washing the dishes is to try to leave the dishes to drip dry in the dish drainer. That way you won't use as many towels, and you'll cut down on the amount of energy you use by loading the washing machine with so many dish towels. It also means that there's one less after-dinner chore for you!

Late Summer Foraging

As squirrels well know, autumn may be the best time of year to forage for wild foods. There are berries, nuts and fruits galore in our woodlands and forests.

Autumn is also the season for mushrooms, although in order to eat those you pick in the wild safely you really need to know your mushrooms. There are thousands of different types of mushrooms and toadstools all flourishing in the fall, and the simple message is: if you aren't absolutely sure about a mushroom, don't eat it. While there are many tasty specimens out there to be enjoyed, there are plenty that can leave you seriously ill, or even cause death. For example, the poisonous Yellow Stainer mushroom can easily be confused with the popular horse chestnut.

Mushrooms are extremely important to their ecosystems—they help to break down dead organic matter—but there are a few rules that prospective mushroom pickers can abide by to make sure their foraging doesn't have an impact on the environment: only pick what you intend to eat, avoid taking button mush-rooms (ones that are yet to expand), and only collect from large populations.

Glorious Auroras

The Northern and Southern Lights, or the Aurora Borealis and Aurora Australis, as they are otherwise known, are possibly the most spectacular visual phenomena that the natural world has to offer. They are natural displays in which beautifully colored washes of light dance across the sky at night. They are most often observed in the polar zones, and most often during the months of September and October in the north.

The flashing and sweeping greens, pinks and blues of the Northern Lights are called Dance of Spirits by the Cree of Canada, although the Northern Lights in particular have had a number of names through time. The science behind them has to do with the collision of electrons in the upper areas of the Earth's atmosphere.

The different colors are caused by a combination of chemicals in the upper atmosphere: oxygen tends to produce the green and red colors, while blue and violet auroras are mainly due to atmospheric nitrogen. Chemistry class never looked as beautiful as these night skies!

September
12

Giving the Gift of Time

Everyone loves to receive a present, but often your friends and family would rather receive a thoughtful gift of time rather than another nice, but often needless, gift of bubble bath, socks or yet another pair of slippers.

Here are a few ways that you could offer up your time, the next time you want to give someone a present they'll remember.

🌸 **Babysitting**: There aren't many parents who wouldn't gratefully receive the offer of childcare for an evening—or even a weekend.

🌸 **Outdoor chores**: A good gift for elderly friends or relatives who struggle keeping their own gardens up to scratch, or can't cope with the lawn or snow removal.

🌸 **Handy helping**: If you are good at carpentry, plumbing or painting, offer to take care of those little jobs that have been put off for ages.

🌸 **Housework**: Busy moms are sure to appreciate someone else doing the dusting and vacuuming!

🌸 **Companionship**: Has your friend always wanted to go to a certain evening class, theater show or museum but has lacked the time or confidence to go it alone? Arrange it for them and then offer up your company too.

September 13

The Wind and the Waves

Renewable energy is the way forward for the sake of the planet's future. Wind power, hydroelectricity and wave turbines need to be the ways in which the majority of energy is created in the near future. The best option is government legislation to encourage utility companies to buy renewable energy and offer competitive tariffs to their customers.

The good news is that many countries understand the need for renewable energy tariffs, and anyone with any doubts about their benefits should only look to Denmark, where they were brought in first, and Germany, where the government has taken the development of renewable energy to the next level.

Aside from building your own wind farm, what can you do to encourage the use of renewable energy? The answer is to ask your energy supplier what their tariffs are for renewable domestic energy. After all, the more interest they have, the more likely they are to offer energy from renewable sources at a competitive rate.

September 14

Clean Up the World Weekend

The third weekend in September is Clean Up the World Weekend, so what better time to organize a local clean-up? The idea behind the weekend is to inspire people and their local communities to make their own small part of the world a cleaner, healthier and more pleasant place to live in.

All it takes to improve your public space is to have a good clean-up. Gather together friends and neighbors, a pile of garbage bags, some heavy-duty utility gloves and a wheelbarrow or two, and you have your clean-up squad ready to roll.

Just remember that Clean Up the World Weekend is not just about getting rid of trash; the idea is also to make sure anything found that can be recycled is recycled, and that anything that could be put to a good use is. And when your clean-up crew is through, not only will you have a much cleaner neighborhood, but you will all experience an improved sense of community spirit as well.

Why not reward your efforts in the neighborhood by having a pot-luck dinner after a hard day's cleaning? Just remember to use local, organic food when possible—and no paper plates!

September 15

A New Look

Being green doesn't mean you need to live in a home that always looks like it needs a good coat of paint; the key to environmental redecorating is to think twice about how you decorate and what products you use.

So here are a few tips while you plan your home's makeover:

❀ Try alternatives to paints filled with harmful chemicals, such as good old-fashioned whitewash, which is made from lime.

❀ Opt for natural products whenever you can, like reclaimed clay tiles, recycled wool carpets and rag rugs.

❀ Revamp and renew your tables, mirrors and picture frames by using broken tiles to make mosaic tops or surrounds.

❀ Opt for sofas, seat coverings, throws and cushions that are made from untreated, unbleached hemp, colored with natural dyes.

❀ Instead of installing a whole new kitchen, your kitchen cupboards can be revamped with a coat of eco-friendly paint and new handles made from recycled materials.

September 16

Ozone day

September 16 has been designated International Day for Preservation of the Ozone since 1994. It began as a way of increasing awareness of the importance of safeguarding the ozone layer, the shield that encircles the Earth, protecting the planet from some of the Sun's harmful radiation.

Ozone is the form of oxygen that is made up of three oxygen atoms, rather the the diatomic oxygen that we breathe. When ultraviolet radiation from the Sun reacts with normal oxygen in the atmosphere, ozone is produced. This radiation-formed ozone layer is vital in order to maintain life on our planet; it acts as a protective barrier. This is why measures were taken to try to prevent further damage, when scientists first discovered that manmade chemicals were destroying the ozone layer, causing serious harm.

An international treaty was signed to preserve the ozone layer, and thanks to the cessation of the manufacturing of chemicals that destroy ozone, the hole in the ozone layer is beginning to shrink. Everyone has to remain vigilant to make sure that no more damage is ever done.

September 17

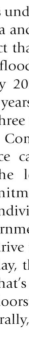

Too Much Water...

Sea levels are rising around the world as a result of the melting ice caps. With this increase, much of the world's coast comes under threat. The UN predicts that by 2010 more than 80 percent of people will be living within 62 miles of a coast and that there are currently 634 million people across the world living in areas in danger of being consumed by the sea in the near future. The low-lying cities under threat include New York, Tokyo, Mumbai, Shanghai, Jakarta and Dhaka.

In worst case scenarios, experts also predict that by 2080 more than 100 million people could regularly be flooded by rising sea waters and—in the very worst scenario—by 2090, megafloods, which normally hit North America every 100 years, could hit every three to four years.

Combating melting ice caps will require the long-term commitments of both individuals and governments. If you can drive to the coast in a day, this is a problem that's right on your doorstep, perhaps literally, so act now!

...Or Too Little?

While citizens of many third-world countries struggle to find enough drinking water to survive, with many relying upon disease-riddled sources, most people in the Western world never stop to think about how much water they use on a daily basis. Even by the time most of us have left the house in the morning we have gone through gallons, thanks to flushing toilets, teeth brushing, showers and washing dishes.

That is why World Water Monitoring Day is so important. Its aim is to encourage people all over the world to think about how much water they use and, by issuing test kits, to ensure that water supplies across the globe meet safety criteria including temperature, clarity and acidity. The day's organizers, the Water Environment Federation and the International Water Association, hope to expand participation to one million people across 100 countries by 2012.

Water is one of our most precious resources, and ensuring that everyone has access to clean water one of our most serious and pressing responsibilities.

To find out more about this, check out the World Water Monitoring Day website.

September
19

Recycled Giftwrap

It's a lovely experience both to give and receive a beautifully wrapped gift, but even the most environmentally friendly of presents can become far from green if the wrapping paper goes straight into the trash. So think about some of these ways you can recycle or reuse your wrapping paper.

❀ Some wrapping paper can be recycled with the newspapers and other paper-based waste by your local authority or recycling center, but you will need to check out your area's regulations.

❀ Try to open your gifts carefully so that you can reuse the wrapping paper for the next present you have to give.

❀ Keep giftwrap, ribbons and attractive string or bows for your children to use to make pictures or greeting cards.

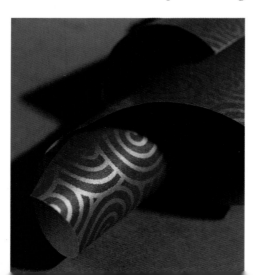

❀ Use as protective cover for books—school and college students often have to cover up their textbooks.

❀ Crumpled sheets of used giftwrap can be great for cleaning windows.

❀ Cut up scraps and off-cuts of giftwrap into small pieces, square or shaped, to use as gift tags.

September 20

Buy Seasonal

Seasonal shopping is a great way of helping the environment, by ensuring that we're not buying foods that have been imported from thousands of miles away to eat out of season. And it's a good way to boost the local economy.

Unsurprisingly, food that has been grown locally tastes far better than that which has been in storage and transit for weeks. After all, which sounds more appealing: a tomato that was picked green, then packed up and shipped hundreds of miles, so that it was already two weeks old when it hit the supermarket shelf, or a piping hot pie made with apples picked yesterday?

Not only does the food taste better, but eating local, seasonal produce dramatically reduces the carbon footprint. Transport, packaging, refrigeration: all of this is vastly reduced when you choose local, seasonal food, and it's better for local producers.

So to help you dish up some tasty autumn recipes, here are a few foods that are seasonal in September.

Bountiful Harvest

- Sweet potatoes, sweetcorn, butternut squash, onions, pumpkins
- Plums, apples, blackberries
- Perch, herring
- Autumn lamb, venison
- Pheasant, partridge, duck

September 21

Wood Nymphs

In ancient Greece, wood nymphs were creatures that lived in springs, by rivers and in valleys, and in some parts of Greece they were still honored in the early 20th century. These mythological entities, which were always in female form, were either tied to a particular place or were part of a god or goddess's followers. Dionysus, Hermes and Pan all had wood nymphs among their groups, as did the huntress Artemis.

In Greek mythology, the marriage between a wood nymph and a patriarch was very common as it lent authority to the king and his ancient line. (The idea of the king making a divine marriage with a female deity dates back to ancient Mesopotamia.) Dryads were the nymphs who made their homes in trees; Heleads were believed to live in marshes; and Oreads lived in the mountains.

Nymph legends occur in many cultures. In poetry, nymphs often appear as free, independent female spirits, able to marry human men at their own volition. Only recently has "nymph" been used as a derogatory word for wanton women.

September 22

International Car-Free Day

Most of us these days are far too reliant on our cars. It is all too easy to jump in and start the engine, to go to work in the mornings, to do the school run or even just to do the morning errands. However, for most of us there are alternatives to driving that we tend to forget about.

International Car-Free Day is an opportunity to explore other options. Who knows, you might even enjoy the break from being stuck behind the wheel on the freeway or in the morning traffic.

Taking the train or bus are both more environmentally friendly ways of getting to the office, and many people live within walking distance of their workplace and children's schools. Walking with your children gives you a chance to spend extra time together.

If you are more adventurous you could even try taking up cycling. One of the best things you'll find is that the trip to work or school also becomes your day's exercise.

So try leaving the car at home today if you can. It may work so well you that want to do it more often.

There is more information about International Car Free Day on the internet.

September 23

In A Jam

Autumn is the perfect time for gathering and foraging, but the best way to make the most of what you collect from your garden or local woodlands is to preserve and store them properly to enjoy later. This is also a great time to stock up at the local farmer's market while prices are low.

Here are a few tips:

❀ Berries and plums can be made into jellies, jams and preserves, ensuring that they will keep all winter.

❀ Apples can be either be stored as they are in a cool, dry place, made into pies and frozen, or even turned into homemade cider.

❀ Mushrooms are another autumn favorite, and fresh mushrooms can be kept for as long as five days if they are stored properly, which means in the refrigerator in a paper bag. Don't wash them until you are ready to use them and avoid storing them in plastic of any kind.

❀ Most winter squash varieties will keep for up to a month, and sweet potato stays good for up to four weeks if it is stored in cool, dry conditions.

Jaws!

Perhaps no other creature on Earth inspires as much fear as a shark. Even though these amazing fish come in all shapes and sizes—the dwarf lantern shark is a mere 7 inches long—it is the image of the fearsome Great White Shark, with its vast mouth of razor-sharp teeth, that endures.

Amidst all the splashing and screaming, it's easy to forget that the shark is an utterly amazing creation. What makes sharks such fearsome predators is their noses and the ability to differentiate one miniscule part of water from the millions of others. By operating at the chemical level they can smell things with astounding accuracy. And while some sharks are solitary hunting creatures, many are social animals and tend to stay together in large schools.

Sharks do occasionally attack humans, although experts are divided on whether or not they ever truly consider humans as prey, but it is the stories of their obvious dislike of dolphins that are most intriguing. One experiment showed that sharks would not attack seals when there was a mechanical dolphin in the water, and many people have reported being "saved" by dolphins when under threat from shark attack.

September 25

Home, Sweet Home

New Zealand has a retrofit home project designed to make housing greener, drier and warmer by installing insulation and clean heating systems. Focusing on the Waitemata district of Auckland (harbor area shown in photo below), the project set out to retrofit 150 low-income homes with energy-efficient measures in order to help reduce inhabitants' energy bills, as well as the country's general fuel consumption.

These homes now have green features such as lagging and insulation, modern, energy-efficient windows, under-floor damp proofing and low-flow showerheads. The project is also beneficial for the community at large, by creating employment and training people who were previously unemployed to do the work.

Governments do care!

While it may be harder for you to get a government grant to retro-fit your entire home, you may be able to make one of these changes on your own. There will be some initial expense, but the heating, cooling and emissions savings will kick in immediately.

September 26

Giving It All Away

Many people have closets full of clothes that they never wear or that their children have outgrown. Sometimes these garments have never even been worn.

As you switch from your summer to winter wardrobe, now is a great time to clean out those closets and liberate some much-needed space. It's also a great way to do your good deed for today.

When you get started on this chore, remember to bag up your unwanted clothes and send them to a charity shop or thrift store. You are reducing your impact on the environment by recycling, while giving a charity the opportunity to raise money from your old clothes so that they can offer a helping hand to the disadvantaged. Of course, it is not just clothes that thrift stores are happy to accept; anything that is lying unwanted (in reasonable condition) in your home could find a new home while raising funds for a good cause.

While you're dropping off your unwanted clothes, why not have a look around the store for some new winter clothes for use in the coming months? If you also buy from a charity shop, you double your environmental benefits.

September 27

The More, The Merrier

Water is one of the hottest topics when it comes to saving our planet. Unless we live in a drought area, we're all guilty of looking on nature's wine as a never-ending resource, but we need to learn to conserve our water supplies, and to think about the energy we consume when heating it.

One way you can cut back on water use is to bathe your younger children together. Not only will you save water and energy, you will also help turn bath time into fun time for your children. With a sibling in to splash with and a few water toys, bath time no longer feels like a chore. As always, make sure you're not using more water than you need. If you fill the tub to the brim, the little ones will only splash it all over the floor, so just go with half.

Children are more interested in the bubbles and toys anyway.

The best part for parents is that it will also cut the amount of time it takes to get through this evening ritual. And if you and your significant other don't have kids, you can still apply the same rule for grown-ups!

September 28

Hug a Veggie!

It may be hard to understand the variety of problems today's mass consumerism inflicts upon the planet. In recent decades, a love of "stuff" has led to a more wasteful society. This is why Green Consumer Day is important as a way of encouraging all of us to reduce, reuse, and recycle. So donate your extra stuff to a charity, choose recycled products, or just skip the usual shopping trip, and reduce your eco-footprint for a day.

September 28th is also International Hug a Vegetarian Day. Even if you are not a vegetarian, it won't hurt to hug one, and encouraging vegetarianism holds benefits for everyone. After all, research shows that vegetarians who still eat milk and eggs have a considerably smaller carbon footprint than meat eaters.

Many vegetarians shun meat because of the way farm animals are kept and slaughtered. Supporting vegetarianism is a vote for animal rights and environmental conservation. And even if you're not inspired to go veggie, you can help by only buying free-range organic meats.

To find out more on both days check out the websites.

September 29

Green Hobbies

As more and more people look for a break from their stressful, work-driven lifestyles, relaxing, old-fashioned and gentler pastimes are becoming more popular.

Many traditional activities are not only more environmentally friendly, they are also better for the body and soul. So to soothe your soul and the planet, consider one of these activities.

❀ Gardening is a great way of helping the environment while also aiding relaxation and keeping physically fit.

❀ If you're feeling active, why not take up cycling, walking or even fishing? Just make sure that river stocks are taken into consideration and everything caught is either thrown back or eaten.

❀ Knitting, embroidery and crochet are time-honored ways of

spending your leisure time without impacting the environment—and producing useful and beautiful things, too.

❀ Cooking a good meal for friends with locally sourced, seasonal ingredients is another way of enjoying the simple life. If you don't know how to cook, start learning now!

September 30

It's For the Birds

Birds are an essential component of our delicate ecosystem, and the closer it gets to winter, the harder life becomes for our feathered friends. Climate change and other human interventions are upsetting the natural balance of resources, and an extra-long winter means that food supplies become scarce. That's why it's a good idea to put out a bird feeder filled with nuts and seeds to help local birds survive the cold months. Don't wait until it's too cold or icy to work outside!

The best news is that feeding birds doesn't need to leave you out of pocket, as you can make your own bird feeder and you don't need any power tools or special equipment.

An empty, well-cleaned milk carton or dish-soap bottle, with part of the side cut out of it, filled with nuts then hung from a tree, makes a workable bird feeder. Sunflower seeds and peanuts, or other seed/nut mixes, are readily available for your feeder.

If you have no outdoor space for a bird feeder, even just leaving crusts of bread on a windowsill will be greatly appreciated by the local birds. Just make sure not to do this in or near wildlife parks, where rangers prefer that people don't feed the birds.

October
1

Walk to School Month

The sometimes onerous task of trying to get the kids off to school is made all the more difficult on cold mornings, as everyone wants to stay in bed just a little bit longer; it becomes all too tempting to jump in the car at the last minute to drop your children off right at the school doors.

That's why the founders of International Walk to School Month came up with the idea in 1994 of encouraging more people to walk to school. Millions of people in dozens of countries around the world take part every year. Walking allows you extra time to talk to your children, and promotes fitness as well as greener ways. See April 8 for more on the benefits of regular walking.

However, walking to school isn't an option for many, who simply live too far away to walk to school. But you can still reduce the

environmental impact of getting your kids to school. Take advantage of school buses, or drop off your child on your way to work. If there are other students who live nearby, make arrangements for carpooling so that each child is not driven individually— remember, you're a parent, not a chauffeur!

No Junk Mail

Junk Mail: No Thanks!

You don't need much awareness of green issues to be horrified by the amount of junk mail that arrives at your home every day. Each mail drop could be filled with unsolicited leaflets, catalogs, offer letters and magazines.

The majority of this unwanted mail can go straight in the recycling bin, but there are ways you can stop junk mail arriving at your house in the first place, which is much better for the environment as it saves energy and resources. In the USA, look up the "Stop Junk Mail" website, which offers a service of blocking 90 percent of unwanted mail; in the UK, the Mail Peference Service performs this service, and similar organizations exist elsewhere.

A good way to reduce your regular mail and save paper is to contact your utility suppliers to find out if they offer online services. That way you can keep on top of your account details and payments through the internet whenever you want, and no longer have a need for paper statements or bills. Most banks now offer online banking, which reduces the need for paper statements too.

October 3

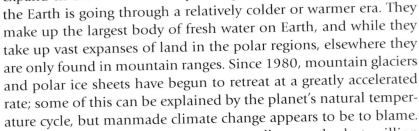

Glaciers

Glaciers are large, frozen rivers or ice sheets that expand in area or retreat depending on whether the Earth is going through a relatively colder or warmer era. They make up the largest body of fresh water on Earth, and while they take up vast expanses of land in the polar regions, elsewhere they are only found in mountain ranges. Since 1980, mountain glaciers and polar ice sheets have begun to retreat at a greatly accelerated rate; some of this can be explained by the planet's natural temperature cycle, but manmade climate change appears to be to blame.

Glaciers have come and gone repeatedly over the last million years, almost completely covering the planet during the world's coldest spells, known as Ice Ages. Excluding the polar regions, glaciers now cover only half the area they did a century ago; they are are in danger of disappearing altogether. And as the ice melts, sea levels will rise and land masses, populations and cities around the world come under threat of vanishing beneath the waves.

The Wild Side

A day for everyone who loves animals, October 4 has been designated World Animal Day (WAD) since 1931. The date was chosen because it is the feast day of St. Francis of Assisi, who was known for his remarkable affinity with animals. Its original goal was to raise awareness of the plight of endangered species; today, people in 65 countries participate.

World Animal Day pledges in its mission statement to celebrate all animal life, and humankind's relationship with animals, and to acknowledge both the diverse roles that animals play in our lives and how they enrich our lives.

Not linked to any single campaign or drive, World Animal Day works to unite all animal-welfare groups under one banner of caring for animals and their habitats. Every year, millions of people around the world take part in events and activities to raise funds for animal-welfare charities.

Check the World Animal Day website to find out how you can add your support.

October 5

Work from Home

While many people would love to work from home every day, most of us have jobs where that simply isn't possible. However, working from home every now and then can help limit the impact you have on the environment. If your job is suitable, here are a few reasons you could suggest to your employer to let you try working at home once a month:

❀ Not having to commute means that you save time (You also save money and have a less stressful morning!)

❀ Working from home provides you with many opportunities to be more environmentally friendly in other ways too, such as limiting your waste, especially if you usually buy packaged food for your lunch and beverages during the day.

❀ Several studies claim that productivity is greater for telecommuters than office-based workers.

❀ Stress levels are lower in home workers than in the workplace.

In addition to these benefits, you'll save money, probably eat more healthily, and enjoy a better work-life balance if you spend less time traveling to and from work. So if your work lends itself to home, why not try it?

Recycling Cardboard

Most households are, by now, pretty good at recycling paper: newspapers, waste computer paper and junk mail usually find their way into the recycling bin. But many paper-recycling points don't accept cardboard, which means that a vast quantity of cardboard ends up in the trash every year.

For non-printed cardboard, you can do something about this yourself by composting it. Make sure that the cardboard has been cleaned of all glue patches, packing tape or staples, and then simply break it up into small pieces and add it to an already established compost heap. There, it will decompose and provide a balance for the "green waste" in your compost. If you don't already have a composter, and you have an outdoor space to start one, see February 17 for more information.

Old corrugated cardboard, which is easy to recycle, can be sold to waste-paper dealers: check for schemes local to you.

In some areas, used cardboard can be converted to fuel for burning as an alternative energy source. Again, check what is available near you.

October
7

How Sweet It Is

Honey has long been used as a natural way to sweeten foods and drinks, but the tasty substance was also known by the ancients to improve a person's wellbeing. So, to help you look at honey in a new light, here are a few reasons why you should keep honey in your pantry:

❀ Eating honey that has been produced from bees in your local area is believed to help protect against hay fever.

❀ Manuka honey from New Zealand has been proven to have medicinal benefits on cuts and sores, thanks to its antibacterial properties, and even to help cure hospital superbugs.

❀ Adding honey to drinks is a healthier alternative to sugar.

❀ Honey is known to boost energy levels, hence its popularity as a breakfast staple.

❀ Eating honey is thought to promote the immune system. A hot drink with a spoonful of honey stirred into it is a time-honored and effective way to relieve symptoms of a cold and sore throat.

Warm and Fuzzy Feelings

Felt is made from sheep's wool that has been roughly spun, beaten and rolled. Thus, it is an entirely natural material that comes from a renewable resource.

That's one reason why wearing slippers made from felt is such a great idea. If you happen to have your own source of pure wool, then it is possible to make your own felt at home. If not, there are plenty of ways of either buying felt to make your own, or buying ready-made felt slippers that are fully environmentally friendly.

Felt slippers are hardly a new idea. Indigenous people all over the world, particularly in Finland and Russia, have long relied on felt footwear—and your own grandparents are likely to have owned a pair of felt slippers in their younger days. In recent years they have become harder to come by. But with our increased awareness of green issues, felt goods, and especially slippers, are making a comeback.

Other felt products that are gaining in popularity include shirts and skirts, purses, placemats and soft toys.

If you're making your own felt, why not go one step further and color it with natural dyes? (For dyes, see September 7.)

October 9

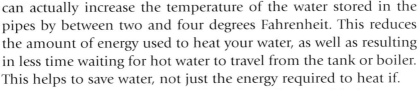

Piping Hot

There are many benefits to insulating your hot-water pipes. Not only does it reduce heat loss, it can actually increase the temperature of the water stored in the pipes by between two and four degrees Fahrenheit. This reduces the amount of energy used to heat your water, as well as resulting in less time waiting for hot water to travel from the tank or boiler. This helps to save water, not just the energy required to heat if.

For these reasons, you should insulate all accessible hot-water pipes, in particular those closest to the water heater, where most heat loss occurs. Pipe sleeves made of polyethylene or neoprene foam can be used for insulation, or, otherwise, you could tape strips of fiberglass insulation around the pipes. If you are using a sleeve, place it over the pipe with the seam down and tie, tape or clamp it every foot or so.

Other ways to conserve hot water include fixing leaks, fitting low-flow devices to shower heads, and making sure that you have the most energy-efficient appliances in your home.

October 10

Going Underground

When it comes to gardening, a little planning ahead is always important. During the fall, when the leaves are turning glorious shades of orange and red and many plants are losing their blooms, it's time to start thinking about what your garden needs to thrive during the following spring and summer. Bulbs and other spring-flowering plants need to be planted out before the ground becomes hard with frost.

Here are a few tips on planting bulbs:

❀ Make sure the area you are planting in is completely clear of weeds and has been given compost or other organic matter.

❀ When buying bulbs, go for plump, firm ones and reject any that have signs of mold or appear to have wasted away.

❀ Bulbs should be planted at a depth of about 6 inches, or roughly twice as deep as the bulb itself (follow any specific instructions that come with the species you're planting).

❀ Squirrels can be the biggest enemy of bulbs, especially in urban gardens. If this is a big problem in your garden, chicken wire will deter them.

❀ Bulbs look better in clumps than sparsely planted. They can be planted in patio pots if you don't have any other space.

October 11

Efficient Heating

With energy bills soaring in recent years, and fears over the amount of carbon dioxide being produced by our use of domestic fuel, it is more important than ever that we heat our homes as efficiently as possible. Here are some tips on the best way of saving energy (and cash!) when it comes to heating your home.

❋ Double glazing and loft insulation reduce the amount of energy you need to heat your home and cut the cost of heating bills.

❋ Installing an energy-efficient boiler could save money quickly: experts estimate that you would recover the cost within five years.

❋ Reducing the temperature on your thermostat by just one degree can reduce heating bills by as much as 10 percent a year.

❋ Almost a third of all heat is lost through the walls. Installing cavity-wall insulation could save you 20 percent on your bills.

❋ Eliminate drafts by fitting brushes in outside doors; sealing windows, using draft excluders/door snakes and insulating under floorboards.

❋ Placing aluminum foil behind radiators can help by reflecting heat back into the room.

❋ If you have a radiator under a window, don't close curtains over it as this will block the heat.

October 12

Toy Libraries

Bowing to the pressure from your child for the latest toy on the market, or the new doll, bicycle or computer game their friends have, can seem irresistible at times. But in reality, how many of your children's toys do they actually play with or use on a regular basis? More often than not, new ones are quickly forgotten and often end up lying around the bedroom, and eventually end up in landfill. For this reason alone, toy libraries are a great idea.

For a nominal fee, toy libraries allow adults to borrow or hire toys and equipment rather than buy them. Your child has access to a regular supply of new toys without you having to splash the cash on filling up their toy boxes with brand new teddy bears, dolls and electronic games that are all too quickly forgotten.

If your community doesn't have a toy library, then why not set one up? All you need is the cooperation of your local library or school and some donations of toys to set up. It is even possible to get grants for this in some places.

To find out more or find a toy library in your area, check on the internet.

October 13

Disaster Reduction

In 2001, the General Assembly of the United Nations decided to maintain the observance of Natural Disaster Reduction Day as a vehicle to promote a global culture of natural-disaster reduction, including disaster prevention, mitigation and greater preparedness. As part of the same resolution, the UN decreed that an International Decade for Natural Disaster Reduction should be introduced, with the aim of limiting the loss of life, property destruction, and social and economic disruption caused by natural disasters.

It is widely accepted that, thanks to global warming, natural disasters have become more frequent in recent years, especially in Asia, which has been hit by a worrying run of floods, tsunamis

and typhoons during the last decade. Hurricanes in North America and the Caribbean have sometimes been especially severe in the 21st century— most notably, Hurricane Katrina's destruction of the New Orleans area.

While long-term measures to stop global warming may help eventually, in the short term it is important that everything possible is done to prepare for whatever weather phenomena the natural world can throw at us.

It Could Be a Prince!

South America's rainforests are teeming with life, and frogs have always been a vital and prolific part of this amazing ecosystem. However, the number of species has been rapidly dwindling, a problem especially seen in Ecuador.

Frogs like the Atelopus Bolengeri—a species endemic to the country in areas 3000 to 6500 feet above sea level but now only known to exist in six localities—are listed as critically endangered. Another Ecuadorean frog, the Atelopus Nanay, was last observed in 1989. Conservationists are now worried that this species of tropical frog has already become extinct.

The World Conservation Union also considers the Phantasmal Poison Frog to be endangered: this species lives only in Ecuador, and its numbers are continuing to drop due to the shrinkage of the habitat it needs for survival. The frog is small, only growing to just over an inch in length at most, with brown or brick-red skin, and usually sports three cream, yellow or light-green stripes running across its head to its rump. And while the poison on this frog's skin is very dangerous, scientists have derived from it the active ingredient for a painkilling drug that is 200 times as powerful as morphine.

October 15

Green Communities

If you live among like-minded people, perhaps a group of you might want to help create a more environmentally friendly community, but don't know how to get started. So why not host a Green Neighborhood Day as a way of inspiring action? All you need to do is invite as many friends and neighbors as possible to an informal meeting to discuss ways in which you could communally improve the neighborhood.

One easy suggestion that can have a big impact is a neighborhood clean-up. Reclaiming unused and neglected places to plant trees or even vegetable gardens are more good ideas you might be able to pursue. All vegetables grown can be shared out.

Organizing a food co-op is another way of becoming more environmentally friendly as a community, or you could even keep goats, chickens or pigs if there is a suitable space for them; the chores can be shared out.

Starting compost and garden-waste shredding schemes are easily shared projects, as are bartering schemes, seed swaps, and car pools.

October 16

World Food Day

With food costs constantly rising, sources diminishing and increasing floods and drought, it is more important than ever that global efforts are made to ensure that all the world's people are properly nourished. Yet many face the prospect of having too little food; the UN's Food and Agriculture Organization, which founded Word Food Day, estimate that in 2009 there are around 963 million people worldwide who are undernourished.

Hunger is worst in the Horn of Africa, but there are an estimated 5 million in Afghanistan, 6.5 million in North Korea, and 38 million (FDA figures) in the USA. According to UNICEF, there are 143 million children worldwide under the age of five who are underweight. World Food Day is designed to raise awareness of the plight of all the world's undernourished people and to attempt to alleviate their suffering.

Talks and exhibitions are organized around the world, and charities ask for volunteers on World Food Day to help with projects for needy countries, to try to provide enough to feed the world's malnourished for at least one day.

To find out more, check the websites of the UN, Oxfam and the International Mercy Corps.

October
17

Green Souvenirs

Favor boxes are a lovely way of saying thank you to wedding guests, as an extra gift for friends and family at anniversary parties, or, of course, for kids' parties. They can mean even more if they are homemade—and making your own means that your favors can be environmentally friendly, too.

Homemade sweets make lovely favors, and you could present them in hand-decorated boxes, made from recycled cardboard. To add an extra touch, the boxes could be decorated with dried flowers or sprigs of seasonal greenery. Handmade pouches make a nice alternative to favor boxes and can just as easily be filled with candy, natural soaps, or even candles. Scent pouches filled with lavender make lovely favors for women.

Party Favor Ideas

✔ Homemade candy for kids: it's healthier than store candy!

✔ Fair-trade, organic chocolate.

✔ Packets of wildflower seeds, or organic herb and veggie seeds.

✔ Natural soaps and scents.

✔ Buy carbon offsets instead of favors for each of your guests.

✔ Get kids to make craft items at the party to take home.

Don't Let It Go down the Drain!

Water left running unnecessarily is always a waste. Not only does it place a strain on natural resources, hot water also takes energy to heat, energy that is wasted when the water is allowed to wash down the plughole unused. In fact, it is estimated that somewhere between 21 and 38 cups of water can be wasted during every minute a tap is left to run! We should all become more aware of the water we use. For men, a large quantity of water can be wasted while shaving.

It's all too easy to let the hot water run as you shave so you can rinse your razor, but it really isn't necessary. The best way to ensure you are only using the amount of water you need is to fill the basin with around two cups of warm water, soak a washcloth in the clean water and then leave it aside to wash your face after your shave. You can use the leftover water in the basin to clean the blade as you go. Having a warm washcloth ready to clean your face is a lovely way to end your shave.

October 19

Baking Soda

Baking soda (or bicarbonate) is among the most useful substances in your kitchen. It can be used instead of most chemical-based cleaning fluids, for a fraction of the price. Here are some tips for using your baking soda.

❧ A mixture of water and soda can be used to wipe stains from washable wallpaper, or to brighten up white furniture.

❧ A tub of water containing two tablespoons of baking soda makes the perfect bath for a dog: it helps remove odors.

❧ Soaking grill pans and roasting tins in a solution of baking soda helps to lift grease. Your pans will rinse out easily after soaking.

❧ Brushing your teeth with baking soda is a great way of bringing up their natural whiteness.

❧ Dusting baking soda on carpets and leaving it overnight can deodorize them; just vacuum the next day.

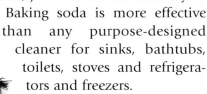

❧ Baking soda is more effective than any purpose-designed cleaner for sinks, bathtubs, toilets, stoves and refrigerators and freezers.

❧ A little baking soda mixed with a cup of vinegar is perfect for cleaning drainpipes too—just pour the mixture down the drain.

October 20

Get the Green Light

Giving up your car is the best thing you can do for the environment, but there are many people who need their cars, yet still care passionately about the state of our planet. The good news is there are plenty of ways in which car users can lessen the impact their driving has on the environment.

When you do need to use the car, make sure you do so as conscientiously as possible. Ask yourself if your journey is necessary, and if so, could you manage on foot, by using public transport, or doubling up with someone else to combine your journeys. Try to opt for routes and times that will be less congested, and carpool with family and friends for commutes and other routine trips.

Don't rev the engine more than necessary, and keep up a steady pace to reduce your fuel consumption. A properly maintained car is more energy-efficient, so have yours serviced regularly (every 3 months or 3000 miles). Ensure that your tires are inflated to the correct pressure. And don't be idle—if you are waiting more than a few minutes, shut off the engine.

October 21

You Are What You Eat

How can you tell if something is really organic? Check the label. Organic farmers and food producers started to use the USDA seal from October 21, 2002. Adoption of the seal is voluntary for certified organic producers, but the appearance of the seal on any product assures customers that the product is at least 95 percent organic.

That means that the seal usually appears on foods such as fruit, vegetables, milk, cheese and other single-ingredient foods. Multi-ingredient foods will only carry the seal if all the ingredients are organic, or at least 95 percent organic. Foods claiming to be made with organic ingredients, but which contain less than 95 percent organic constituents, are not allowed to carry the USDA seal.

According to the European Union, food can only be called

organic if the place where the products were grown is listed, and no genetically modified ingredients are allowed. Only foods that can claim to be at least 95 percent organic can carry the EU's certified-organic logo, but other products can claim to use organic ingredients.

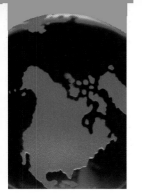

One World Week

Every year millions of people mark One World Week, whose motto is "Hungry for One World," and which occurs in the third week of October. It was founded in 1978 by the World Development Movement to draw attention through local communities to the many diverse cultures that live side-by-side on our planet. OWW's organizers believe that: "When we understand each other's perspectives, our lives can be transformed and enriched."

Its main aims are: to bring people from different backgrounds together to learn about global justice and to spread that learning by working together to care for the Earth and her resources; taking action for justice, equality, peace and fullness of life for all; and building relationships of mutual respect that cross boundaries.

The Bantu (Zulu) word *ubuntu* is central to OWW's work: it is best translated as "active togetherness."
To join in, or even organize, a local event to celebrate ethnic and religious diversity, contact the OWW head office, where someone will put you in touch with a regional co-ordinator.

October 23

Tree Planting

There are any number of reasons why it is a good idea to plant trees, even if it's just one in your own back yard. For a start, not only do trees provide a home to many different kinds of wildlife, they help clean the air, provide shelter from wind and sun, and help save on heating and cooling costs. And of course, they add beauty and color wherever they grow, particularly during the spectacular displays of fall leaves.

Unless you have a space of your own, you may think there is little you can do to encourage the planting of trees. But there are many schemes you can participate in, whether government-led or initiated by corporations attempting to be more green by offsetting carbon emissions with new plantings. You can also make

donations to a host of green charities that promise to plant your tree in return for a regular payment. But the most rewarding way to get involved is to seek out available public spaces in your area, get together with some friends and neighbors and start to plant out a whole new woodland to be enjoyed for generations to come.

October 24

Trading in Hours

When members of a Massachusetts community decided they wanted to turn to bartering as an alternative to hard cash, they simply devised their own, new currency. In Provincetown, at the tip of Cape Cod, one gold dune doubloon represents one hour of time, while a silver one is worth half an hour. To get members started, they are allocated five doubloons when they register with the bartering scheme.

The dune doubloons are one community's way of dealing with low-wage jobs, the lack of low-cost housing and the expense of living within their particular community. With bartering, people can access goods and services—from yard work to accounting—that they might not otherwise be able to afford, while taking the opportunity to earn their own doubloons by using their own particular skills and talents.

Among the most successful and celebrated local currency systems is the Ithaca Hours, in Ithaca, New York, which also involves local businesses and has inspired many similar schemes (see also July 3).

October 25

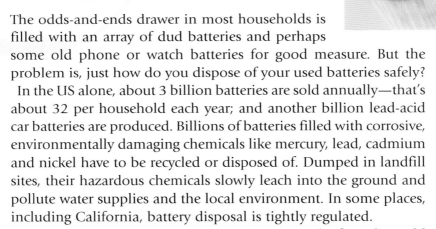

Recycling Batteries

The odds-and-ends drawer in most households is filled with an array of dud batteries and perhaps some old phone or watch batteries for good measure. But the problem is, just how do you dispose of your used batteries safely?

In the US alone, about 3 billion batteries are sold annually—that's about 32 per household each year; and another billion lead-acid car batteries are produced. Billions of batteries filled with corrosive, environmentally damaging chemicals like mercury, lead, cadmium and nickel have to be recycled or disposed of. Dumped in landfill sites, their hazardous chemicals slowly leach into the ground and pollute water supplies and the local environment. In some places, including California, battery disposal is tightly regulated.

So, instead of sending old batteries to landfill, it is important to recycle them safely. This involves a little more work than sending bottles to the recycling bank. In the US and Canada, battery manufacturers have funded a joint recycling center with local depots nationwide. Look for a suitable scheme near where you live.

Sustainable Wood

Wood is a great natural building material, but choosing the wrong wood can have a serious impact on the environment by contributing to the destruction of forests. Tropical rainforests in particular are home to at least half the world's animal species, but more than 1½ acres of rainforest are destroyed every second. Deforestation accounts for as much "greenhouse effect" as all the world's cars, planes, trains and buses.

Picking the right kind of wood for building and furnishings means that you are saving energy at the production stage; it will also be durable and recyclable. To make sure you are buying sustainable wood, always look for the Forest Stewardship Council (FSC) certification, as this standard guarantees that approved wood and paper come from sustainable sources.

If you are buying products that do not carry the FSC logo, try to avoid tropical hardwood products, such as mahogany, teak, rosewood and ebony; these woods are often used to make musical instruments, furniture and other household goods. There are plenty of alternatives that do not call for a trip to tropical rainforests.

October 27

Apples and Pears

One of the joys of this time of year is the ripening of apples and pears. Seeing them mature on orchard trees is a welcome sign that the harvest season is in full swing. You don't even need to head out into the countryside to enjoy the fruit: in many of the busiest cities there are apple and pear trees growing, often with their delicious fruits left to rot, forgotten or ignored.

While a fresh pear or apple eaten straight from the tree is hard to beat, these autumn fruits are just as tasty when made into a range of edible delights that can keep you going through the winter—if no one eats them first, that is! The next time you see a tree laden with precious fruit, imagine the apple crumble or hot pear dessert you could make with it. Or you could make preserves and chutneys to add a fruity zing to meals during the winter months. If you're more adventurous, you could even try your hand at making your own cider: it's just as delicious whether made with the season's best apples or pears.

October 28

Mining

The scale of the global mining industry is greater than most people realize; bear in mind that virtually any natural substance that cannot be grown is mined. Salt, tin, copper, iron, coal, gold, silver and diamonds all need to be excavated, usually from deep underground. People have been mining stone for thousands of years. Gold was mined as early as 2500 BC by the Egyptians, and the Romans developed mining methods that are comparable to those we use today.

Over the course of history, and especially with our recent levels of population and consumption, extensive mining has seriously damaged the environment, both during the mining process and after, when the land is reclaimed for other uses. Erosion, chemical contamination of groundwater and reduced biodiversity are common problems, not to mention the unsightly mess left behind.

Most developed nations have now taken steps to regulate the industry to lessen the impact of mineral excavation on the environment.

Mining operations are usually subject to close scrutiny, and disused mining sites are returned to as close as possible to their original state.

October 29

Coffee Revolution

Whether grabbing your morning pick-me-up or meeting someone over a cup of your favorite brew, all those cups of coffee add up. Americans down 400 million cups of coffee each year, while 60 million Italians consume an amazing 14 billion espressos! The most damaging aspect of buying a cup of coffee is the waste that comes with it: paper or styrofoam cups, napkins, plastic spoons, sugar packs—they're all disposable!

The best way to green your cup of java is to make it at home. Instead of a throwaway paper cup, use a mug (if you drink several cups a day, just refill the same one all day). Buy only unbleached, compostable paper filters, and try to use fair-trade, organic, or shade-grown beans. As with any appliance, when buying a new

coffee maker, look for energy-efficient, long-lasting models. To cut down on water and energy waste, consider a single-cup version if you don't share a kitchen with other coffee fans.

If tea is your beverage of choice, you can use these same tips for a fully "green" green tea.

Waterworks

Most people probably don't realize how much water they consume during the working day. How often do workers help themselves to cups of water from the water cooler only to drink a few sips and then leave the rest on a desk somewhere? Think about the amount of water you use for washing hands, flushing toilets, even cooking, if there is a kitchen in your building. If you're in industry, lab research, or other specialist facilities, your workplace may have other water requirements.

Follow these tips to reduce water waste at work:

❀ Remember, and encourage your fellow workers, to avoid wasting water that has been specially cooled in the water cooler; this will save energy as well as water.

❀ Ask the person responsible for maintenance to introduce dual-flush toilets—they only use about half the water of a regular one.

❀ Ask, too, about installing low-flow faucets.

❀ Checking for leaks in pipes, taps and toilets can save thousands of gallons each year.

❀ Ask cleaners to not leave faucets or hoses running while they clean or rinse, as this can waste more than 5 gallons of water per hour.

October 31

Halloween Decorations

There is no need to buy cardboard skeletons, rubber bats and toy witches' hats when it comes to Halloween. It is almost as easy to create a spooky atmosphere and scare (or entertain) your trick-or-treaters with your own homemade crafts, without wasting money and ending up with a pile of paper and cardboard that you might not be able to recycle.

Pumpkins are the obvious place to start—and don't forget to make some delicious pumpkin soup with the soft flesh that is so often discarded. Roasting the pumpkin first adds flavor.

Homemade pancakes dripping in treacle make great party props; the same applies to caramel apples and bowls of apples in water for dunking—add some red food coloring for an extra ghoulish touch!

Use up old white sheets to make ghosts to hang from the ceilings and banisters, and black tissue paper to make spooky bats. Stretched cotton wool can be made into cobwebs to make your home look just like a haunted house.

The morns are meeker than they were,
The nuts are getting brown;
The berry's cheek is plumper,
The rose is out of town.

The maple wears a gayer scarf,
The field a scarlet gown.
Lest I should be old-fashioned,
I'll put a trinket on.

—Emily Dickinson, *Nature 27: Autumn*

November
1

Mexican Day of the Dead

Dia de los Muertos is marked in a number of Central and South American countries, as well as by Hispanic communities in the USA and Canada. It's a time for fondly remembering departed friends and family. Graves are visited and food, flowers and lights are placed on them. What could be a sad event is usually transformed into a joyous celebration.

It can be difficult to think about your last wishes or discuss them with your nearest and dearest, but it is a responsible option that will provide clarity once you are gone. It's also a chance to make plans that really reflect what's important to you. Consider a wicker, bamboo or cardboard coffin, rather than a hardwood option. There are increasing choices of natural sites where burials

are permitted, such as woodlands, not just cemeteries. You might have a tree planted in your memory, or that of a loved one.

Making a will gives you the chance to keep doing good, not just for family and friends, but for the wider community, future generations and the planet after you're gone.

Big Cats

It can be hard to believe that the docile domestic tabby is a distant relative of the cheetahs, lions and tigers that roam across African plains. Big cats are among the most impressive and captivating creatures on earth.

Take the cheetah, for example. With enlarged heart, lungs and nostrils, these animals are built for speed. They can go from 0 to 70 mph in about three seconds, faster than a sports car.

It's not for nothing that lions are known as kings of the jungle. With a roar that can be heard five miles away, and consuming 60 lbs of meat in a single sitting, they are pretty powerful beasts.

Leopards are among the most widespread of big cats. As excellent climbers, good swimmers and stealthy hunters, they are well adapted to their habitat. Leopard markings vary to make best use of local camouflage possibilities, so black leopards, or panthers, have evolved to live in forested areas, while snow leopards are a rare and elusive creature found in colder regions.

A number of big cat species are, however, endangered creatures, threatened with extinction by a combination of creeping habitat loss and hunting.

November 3

Green Volunteering

Sometimes trying for a greener lifestyle can feel like a big list of "don'ts": don't fly, don't drive, don't use chemicals, don't pollute. But you can also do something positive for the environment by volunteering your time.

There are lots of different possibilities for green volunteering to match your interests and availability, from week-long eco-camps to a regular session in a local park or forest. Sometimes it's possible to find a one-off opportunity for a communal project, like a beach clean-up or tree planting day.

The benefits usually include plenty of fresh air, exercise and the chance to meet new, like-minded people. If you sign up to go regularly, you will usually have the chance to do a variety of different

tasks. Plus, it's a chance to pick up new skills. If you want to learn to look after your own garden, what better way to learn from the experts than to help out at an organic farm or heritage garden?

Your local volunteer bureau or community center might have a list of suitable organizations.

November
4

The Humble Spud

The humble potato is often underrated. Not only is it a nutritious and tasty food, the world's number four food crop and the most popular vegetable, but it comes in hundreds of varieties, from violet to golden. It can be served in countless delicious ways: baked, boiled, sautéed, roasted, fried.

This wonderful tuber contains protein, fiber and a good dose of Vitamins C and B. The United Nations recognizes the importance of the potato: 2008 was the International Year of the Potato.

Unlike rice or grains, there are potato varieties that will thrive in virtually every climate. The potato produces more food, more quickly than any other major crop, and they are not usually shipped far, making them a local staple for many. You can even grow spuds in specially designed sacks on your patio.

What better way to celebrate the potato than to eat it? Try these baked fries.

Home-made Fries

Preheat the oven to 500°F. Peel and slice four baking potatoes, ⅛ inch thick. Pat dry and spread on a buttered baking sheet. Brush with butter (or sunflower oil). Bake for 15–20 minutes until edges brown. Sprinkle with salt, or experiment with other flavors.

November 5

Beautiful Glass Bottles

If you have a bottle that's too attractive to recycle, use it to brighten up your décor. You could use it for storing oil in your kitchen—buy a cork with pouring spout for a few cents from a hardware store.

An unusual bottle may be nice enough simply to place on a windowsill, catching the light, as an everyday ornament. And ever since the 1970s, people have been using bottles as candle holders, decades of wax dripping down in the neck in interesting patterns.

For something a little more permanent, you can make your bottle into a lamp. Kits containing a plug of cork or rubber for the neck, all the light-fitting pieces and cord are available from hardware, lighting and craft stores. You can drill the bottle to hide the

cord inside if you have a suitable bit, though it obviously requires care to avoid breaking the bottle. Jazz up an old lampshade with pieces of fabric or ribbon to top it off.

Even plain glass can be made ornamental. Decorate the outside of jars with acrylic paint for colorful candle holders.

After-effects of War

Long after the guns stop firing, the environmental damage from conflicts may continue to hurt people. Debris, unexploded bombs and toxic waste are some of the obvious signs, but damage to water and sewage supplies, abandoned fields and fires can take many years to repair. Today is the international day dedicated to preventing the exploitation of the environment in war and armed conflict. In these chaotic situations, it can be hard to protect the natural world from damage. But restoring the damage caused afterwards can be a priority for the armies involved and international organizations. A tank left rusting in a field could pollute the water supply for decades if it's simply abandoned there, or be a hazard for children at play. Removed, it could be stripped of useful parts and disposed of safely.

Of course, there are many, many good reasons to have fewer wars, but this serves as another reminder that short-sighted human actions can have far reaching effects on the world we live in. In 2007, eight mountain gorillas found shot dead in the Democratic Republic of Congo were believed to have been killed by soldiers. These incidents countered years of conservation efforts.

November
7

Compacting

If you find it hard to bypass the mall, you might find it challenging just reading about Compacters!

In January 2006, ten San Francisco friends decided to turn their backs on consumerism and buy nothing for a year. The environmental impact of buying and discarding so many things was a key motivator. Apart from food, drink and health necessities, they would barter, borrow or acquire everything they needed second-hand. An internet community emerged of others already living a shopping-free existence, or inspired to do so. Even after the allotted year, many found they were much more resourceful than before and couldn't go back to their old shopping ways.

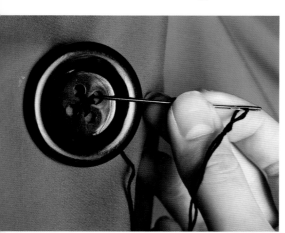

The experience of the Compacters poses questions about what we need to live happily, and challenges why so many people believe they'll find the solutions to their woes in the mall. When considering purchases this week (or month, or year), ask yourself: "Do I really need it?" You may also find their ideas for making do and mending an inspiration.

November 8

Baby It's Cold Outside

As the nights draw in, it's time to plan for winter warmth. Simple steps will keep our heating working efficiently throughout the cold months, and it's wise to plan ahead before it gets too cold.

Bleed your radiators if you hear any knocking sounds when you turn on your central heating: they should run noiselessly and work more effectively. While you're at it, install thermostatic radiator valves, which measure the temperature in the space around the radiator and adjust accordingly; and source reflectors to fit behind the radiators, to bounce the heat back into the room.

If there are any rooms that you don't use often, turn the radiators down to save energy that would be wasted. Get your boiler serviced, to keep it in tip-top condition and maintain efficiency.

Pull your warm clothes out of storage. Find a cozy blanket to keep at hand in the living room for cold nights in front of the fire or television. It will cost you no effort at all to reach for it to cuddle up in, rather than to get up and turn the heating up. Draft-proof your home with sealants on windows, thick curtains and draft excluders ("door snakes": see January 29).

November 9

Algae

Those simple water-dwelling organisms, algae, can be an environmental peril or a sustainable fuel for the future, depending on which way you look at them.

Algae are the basis of many marine food chains, but when water contains too many algae nutrients, for example from pollution, they can multiple fast and furiously. They starve other plants of oxygen and room, killing them. Fish and insects also struggle to survive: they too move out or die, leaving a dead area.

Researchers have spent decades working out how to derive a usable fuel from algae. The aquatic plants store solar energy in a kind of oil, producing up to thirty times more energy per acre than other biofuels. There is no need to dedicate farm land for them.

There is a long way to go to produce usable fuel from these tiny plants in a safe and affordable way, but rising oil prices have given new impetus to the search. In 2009, Continental Airlines made the first flight using an algae-powered jet: a 50/50 mix of ordinary fuel and oil derived from algae.

November 10

Green for Green

When you save or invest money, a typical bank will lend your hard earned cash to whoever they like—it could be a petrochemical company or an arms dealer. But if you choose ethical banking, your money could provide much-needed finance to create wind turbines or organic farms.

There are two kinds of ethical banking. One screens out all the nasties (this might include cigarette manufacturers and companies that test on animals—it depends on their particular ethical code) and lends to everyone else. In the other model, the bank chooses the kind of ethical enterprise they want to support. Some accounts are specifically green, supporting environmental projects.

You may be offered lower interest rates for ethical products, but not necessarily. Eco-friendly products and renewable energy initiatives can be very lucrative! And you're putting your money where your mouth is, so that it's working for the kind of world you want and not financing something you consider unethical.

Some mainstream banks offer ethical products. Let the bank know that you care where they invest, and if you do decide to leave for a more ethical option, tell them why, in writing.

November 11

Voyage of the *Beagle*

Little did the young naturalist Charles Darwin know, as he set off aboard the *Beagle* for a five-year survey of the southern hemisphere, that the journey would set in motion his enquiring mind, ultimately to make history.

Darwin's meticulous collection of plant, animal, insect and fossil samples, and search for an explanation for the huge, surprising diversity he found, shaped how we understand the natural world.

It's hard for us to imagine today the amazement that must have been felt by Darwin's peers at his extensive catalogue of living things. Before the days of foreign travel and wildlife documentaries, such creatures were beyond their wildest imaginings. The work of early naturalists helped show how incredibly diverse, complex and interconnected our world and its creatures are.

When Darwin returned from his epic voyage, the work was by no means over; it had scarcely even begun! It took him a further 20 years of study before his seminal work on evolution, *On the Origin of the Species by Natural Selection*, was ready for publication.

November 12

A Lasting Impression

Taking up the green lifestyle is about more than just having that warm and fuzzy feeling of doing a good deed a day—it's about permanently changing our lifestyle to make a healthier world for now and the future. That is one of the guiding principles behind permaculture.

Permaculture is "permanent agriculture," or natural agricultural systems that can be sustained indefinitely, designed to mimic nature's ways as much as possible. Instead of intensive monoculture, diverse crops and animals are reared, using only renewable energy. Perennial trees and plants grow alongside animals, all the elements naturally complementing one another, with nothing going to waste and no chemical fertilizers added. (See also March 28 for companion planting).

Permaculture isn't limited to those who have acres of land or unlimited budgets. Even if you live in the city, there is a lot you can do with a small garden, or even just pots, windowboxes and a wormery. In Havana, Cuba, 50 percent of the food consumed by residents is grown within the city limits. There are permaculture projects from Afghanistan to Zimbabwe. Get involved in something near you.

November 13

Rainforests

It can be hard to fully comprehend the importance of rainforests for the planet. These forests are true biological treasures, responsible for 20 percent of the oxygen we breathe and absorbing much of the carbon we emit.

Half of all plant, animal and insect species are found in tropical rainforests. One hectare (about 2½ acres) may be home to 750 tree varieties and 1,500 plants; this area will yield 3,000 different fruits —just imagine the fruit salad!

Rainforests may be distant, exotic habitats, but we use many products every day that are derived from them. Where would we be without rubber, coffee, or chocolate? An amazing one quarter of all pharmaceuticals are based on Amazonian plants.

You know what's coming— the rainforest and all these benefits are under threat. More than one acre is lost every second, and at that rate, it will all be gone in 40 years.

Saving the rainforest makes economic sense, too. Left intact and sustainably harvested, the value of an acre of rainforest far outstrips the value of land if cleared for farming.

Slow Food

The fast-food burger or store-bought ready meal is convenient, but that's about all that can be said for either. It takes time, effort and love to bring proper ingredients together in a nutritious and delicious feast.

The Slow Food International Movement was founded in Italy in the 1980s to reclaim good food. These eco-gastronomes believe that food should be about quality, not quantity or speed. A meal should be an event, not simply the fastest way to get nutrients down your throat or assuage your hunger pangs.

Slow Food celebrates good, clean and fair food, produced in harmony with the environment, rather than damaging it. The right of workers to a fair wage is central—our bargain bucket shouldn't be at the expense of exploiting someone else—so a spin-off network of small rural producers, Terre Madre, emerged.

The movement seeks to educate people's taste buds again, after years of living on cheap, nasty food. They also work in schools, helping to set up gardens and open the eyes of children to where their food comes from and how it should be enjoyed.

November 15

Craft Treasure Trove

Conscientious recyclers will always be left with odds and ends that just don't fit in any of the neat categories. Or little scraps of this and that which could surely be put to some use, but what?

Well, it's time to start your recycled crafts box, a home for all those miscellaneous items waiting for a creative use. This is especially useful if you have children (make sure everything is safe).

To make the difference between a box of clutter and a treasure trove for your crafts, keep it in good order, don't hold on to too many of anything until you can think of a use and go for a small-ish box that can be frequently cleared out.

You may like to hoard: off-cuts of fabric and wrapping paper;  empty thread spools; single buttons; pretty ribbons or colorful string; small containers for paint or glue; odd socks or old tights; old plastic cutlery or wooden chopsticks; cardboard; sponge; feathers; corks; shoelaces; bits and pieces from packaging with interesting textures or patterns… and more!

GEOTHERMAL
HEAT PUMPS

EXTRACT HEAT FROM THE
GROUND FOR FREE. HEAT
YOUR BUILDING FOR AS
LOW AS :
2000 SQ/FT $ 550 /YR
3000 SQ/FT $ 800 /YR

Geothermal Power

You may be largely unaware of the energy potential below the ground. But right under your very feet is a free heat source that has the potential to cut your bills and your reliance on fossil fuels.

Geothermal power makes use of the natural heat below the earth's surface. Dig down several feet and the ground is a fairly constant temperature, while the air temperature plummets in winter. To harness this heat, loops of pipe are buried in the ground and left to warm up. With the aid of a pump, the heat stored in the pipes can be transferred from the ground to heat underfloor pipes, radiators or a hot water tank in homes.

It does cost a little electricity to power the pump, but CO_2 savings each year can be as high as six or seven tons, if you are replacing an electric or solid fuel heat source. If you are considering geothermal power, it's worth knowing that you need a little space and suitable ground for a trench or hole to be dug. It works best with an underfloor heating system and is cheapest to install when constructing a new building.

Geothermal power has also powered small substations and commercial greenhouses.

November 17

Now You're Cooking!

We are regularly told that drinking lots of water is a healthy habit. But much of the water we use in the kitchen is a by-product of cooking rather than for consumption. These simple tips for cutting down will save plenty of water without any damage to your cuisine. Heating water takes lots of energy too, so using a little less will save money and power as well.

❀ Wash vegetables in a bowl rather than under a running tap, and pour the water on the garden or pot plants when you are done.

❀ Many vegetables and fish wrapped in foil can be steamed, with just a little water in the bottom of a pan, or steamed over another pot you are boiling.

❀ When boiling potatoes, pasta or vegetables, choose the right size of saucepan and put in just the amount of water you need to cover your food.

❀ Rather than adding lots of water to evaporate when you are making stews and sauces, start by adding a little less and using a lid.

❀ Use an electric kettle; this staple of British kitchens is a great way to make tea and an economical way to boil water for cooking.

Eco-Elegance

If you are hosting or helping with this year's Thanksgiving dinner, you will no doubt want the table to be as festive and special as the food you're serving.

You could opt for an edible centerpiece, such as a fancy bowl or basket piled high with fruit, vegetables and nuts to symbolize the plentiful harvest you're all gathering to celebrate. Create a feast for the eyes with different colors, textures and sizes of produce, like squash, apples and sweet corn. Best of all, your decorative centerpiece can be eaten over subsequent days, leaving no waste behind.

Alternatively, use dry or fresh flowers, nuts, berries and autumn leaves for something smaller or for individual place settings. For placeholders, make small scrolls tied with ribbon or homemade envelopes containing notes of things for which we are thankful.

Choose linen napkins that can be reused, instead of paper ones, plus a fabric table runner for a more luxurious feel. Look out for traditional tableware, full of character, in thrift stores if you need something new, or extra plates for all the guests.

Don't forget: to choose a free-range, heritage turkey, not only kinder on the bird but with better quality meat, suitable for the occasion!

November 19

A Stitch in Time...

Be honest—how many garments in your closets and drawers are in need of repair? In our throwaway society, our first thought is not always repair.

Today is the day to pick out garments needing some TLC and patch up your clothing collection. Mending a tear never takes as long as you fear it will, and taking major or complex repairs to a tailor will be much cheaper than buying a new one.

That old adage, "A stitch in time saves nine," is very true: looking after our clothes will ensure they last longer and in great shape. It also saves resources: even if you recycle the damaged items, energy is needed to grow, make and ship a replacement.

If you aren't very handy with a needle and thread, ask someone to show you how to do simple jobs like replacing a button or darning holes in sweaters. Borrow a sewing machine for hemming or shortening trousers or skirts.

Extend the life of your shoes by polishing regularly, and get them reheeled when they are worn.

Diaper Dilemma

New parents have so much to think about that the green living may come pretty far down the list of priorities. But how you keep your little pride and joy in diapers can make a big difference to the environment.

Disposable diapers are undoubtedly convenient—toss the used ones and forget about them. A sobering thought, though, is that they will still be around in hundreds of years. These "disposable" baby items produce millions of tons of landfill each year.

Biodegradable and bamboo disposables are increasingly available, and while they cost a little more, they create so much less waste that you may consider it a price worth paying. The fact remains that keeping a baby in disposable diapers of any kind costs thousands by the time they are potty trained.

We tend to forget that reusable diapers were the norm just a generation or two ago. Velcro, machine washable and waterproof outer layers make modern reusables much easier to manage than the traditional type.

Services offering to collect and launder your diapers, delivering fresh ones to your door, are increasingly common. It is convenient and it's much, much greener.

November 21

Plenty of Fish in the Sea?

There is definitely something fishy about how humans have exploited the oceans in the last few decades. Today is World Fisheries Day, but without sustainable practices, this nutritious, delicious food could soon become a thing of the past.

Wild-caught fish, swimming freely until the moment they are plucked from the sea by a fishing line or scooped up in a net—it sounds pretty tasty and environmentally friendly. But the shift from small fishing boats to industrial catches has stripped the sea of most large fish, like halibut, marlin, swordfish and tuna.

Which fish are better to eat depends on where you live. The Marine Stewardship Council offers a list (and a logo) for species that are not in crisis. It's important not to stick to the most famil-

iar fish (you have probably heard of them because so many have been caught!) Be prepared to experiment: ask your fishmonger how to prepare unfamiliar types.

Farmed fish may not sound so appetizing, but carefully and sustainably managed, it can be a better option that allows our planet's wild stocks to recover.

Fun Campaigning

You know how important it is to make the changes to improve the environment, but how do you get everyone else on board? Telling them how wrong they are and how they have to change their wasteful ways is probably the worst approach (did that ever work on you?) Instead, lead by example, and make sure people see the good in being green.

While campaigning for change to avert disasters like those that occurred in Chernobyl, Ukraine (see April 26), or Bhopal, India (see December 3), is definitely a good thing, many people are too far away or too young to fully understand the seriousness of these situations. So, start small and local. It would make more of an impact if you organized a push for the local authorities to provide more recycling options. Or perhaps you could focus your efforts on turning unused ground into a park or community garden.

Once you can demonstrate the improvements that people can make when they work together, and show that they can enjoy themselves in the process, your neighbors will be more willing to adopt greener lifestyles and to campaign for change.

November 23

Pass It On!

It's often been said that we need to do a better job of looking after the environment for the sake of future generations. Another important task is bringing our children up to realize just how precious our planet is.

With children's natural curiosity and many natural wonders right there in your own backyard or neighborhood, thankfully this education in the wonders of the world is a pretty enjoyable task.

Kids will probably love to get involved in gardening and composting—after all, those wriggly bugs are pretty exciting for young children. Give them their own small patch or a windowbox to grow crops by themselves and they'll feel so proud of what they produce. This will help them to understand more about where

their food comes from and enjoy eating what they've grown themselves. As they get older, consider letting them keep chickens, or, if you're in a city, take them to urban farms.

Instead of giving in to their appetite for fast food and more "stuff," why not try an picnic lunch followed by a hike outside?

Invasive Species

An invasive species is one that is introduced accidentally or deliberately to a habitat where it does not naturally occur, and gets out of control. Cats brought by settlers to New Zealand kill native birds, while the Melaleuca (paperbark) trees that were introduced from Australia to Florida are destroying the Everglades ecosystem. Sometimes new species are introduced for apparently good reasons—for farming, to replace felled trees, or to "correct" a "problem," as with the paperbark (photo above), which was introduced to reduce "excess" groundwater.

Such species become invasive when they start to thrive and then change the carefully balanced habitat where they have arrived. Often they out-compete native species, using up resources. The invaders don't pose the same problems on home turf, where other creatures or plants provide a balance. Knapweed from eastern Europe produces chemicals harmful to other plants in the American West. But other plants in its home ecosystem are not affected in the same way.

Problematic accidental introductions include the Asian longhorned beetle, which has devastated hardwood trees, and zebra mussels, causing the loss of native marine species.

November 25

More Than Just Tofu

Many would find a juicy steak more appetizing than a tofu burger, but it's really worth giving vegetarian cuisine a second glance, both for your health and the environment. Those unaccustomed to vegetarian cooking and eating are often unaware of the tasty delights they're missing out on.

Some argue that the only sustainable diet is a vegetarian one. Cattle, for example, need more than 10 lbs of food and 13,000 gallons of water for each pound of meat, though other meats are less resource-intensive. That food, or equivalent crops, could be eaten by humans directly, going much further to feed the population.

However, farm animals can graze on land that can't be used for crops, like sheep on rocky or hilly territory. If you can't live without meat, enjoying organic, grass-fed meat a couple of times a week is much better than eating cheaper, poor-quality meat every day.

Vegetarian food doesn't have to be dull! Many of your favorite dishes can be made veggie by replacing the meat, so you can still enjoy your plate of lasagna, chili, or curry.

November 26

Buy Nothing Day

Can you remember the last day that you didn't buy anything? Didn't enter a store or café, or shop online? Near the end of November falls Buy Nothing Day—a single day in which participants keep their wallets closed and escape the grip of the consumerism that seems to be all-pervasive.

Coming just before the biggest shopping period of the year, it's a chance to feel free of this materialism and remind ourselves that we shop to live, not live to shop. It also serves as a reminder of the impact shopping makes on our environment.

There's an environmental impact every time the cash register rings—energy and materials, and probably plenty of oil, go into everything we buy. Most of us are not able to live a shop-free lifestyle, nor would we want to. But there is no harm in taking one day to consider what we buy and how we shop.

Buy Nothing Day is marked by people all over the world, who for at least one day want to be more than just customers. Some like to use the time they might have spent shopping doing something different, inspiring and fun instead. See November 7 to find out how the Compacters spent an entire year buying nothing.

November 27

Green Gadgets

Many people get a thrill out of owning the latest gadgets, but these can be power-guzzling items. There is a whole range of greener gadgets of all types, made from recycled materials, rechargeable or powered by renewable energy.

If you are buying a camera or music player, opt for one that can be recharged rather than being reliant on batteries.

As technology develops, small devices can accommodate a miniature solar panel, which can provide the power. If you like to use your laptop on the go, invest in a solar-powered backpack—it will recharge your computer while you are on the move.

Solar powered or wind-up phone chargers, radios and shavers are also on the market and would make excellent gifts. And there's no need to worry about running out of batteries on your camping trip if you have your wind-up flashlight and solar-powered lantern.

Not only will you be the height of eco-hip, but you can keep these gadgets indefinitely and you'll be saving on electricity and batteries too.

Saving Water, Growing Crops

Clean water and good sanitation are in short supply in many parts of Mozambique. In the remote northern Nissau province, water charities organized a trial of composting latrines—with spectacular results.

The two-pit toilets provided safe, hygienic and permanent sanitation facilities for villagers. Soil and ash were added to the chamber until it was full, then it was blocked up and allowed to compost while the other chamber was used.

The rich, organic fertilizer was then spread on fields, and farmers had a bumper crop. Unlike expensive artificial fertilizers, which ate into their meager incomes and limited the amount of land that could be cultivated, the organic compost from the latrines actually improved soil quality. It held water better and retained its nutrients. The yield from one village's farmland was tripled, thanks to the free fertilizer, and extra crops could be sold to help pay for clothes and schooling.

International charity Water Aid and local partner Estamos were bombarded with requests from other villages wanting to learn how it was done.

November 29

Knitting and Needlecrafts

Old-style needlecrafts are making a welcome comeback. No longer the preserve of grandmothers, with today's trendy patterns you can crochet your favorite cartoon characters or knit your own fashion, or go completely solo and design your own one-of-a-kind creations.

Knitting, crochet, sewing, embroidery and patchwork allow you to make lots of items for your own use or for unique, thoughtful gifts. Starting small, like making gloves, scarves or cushion covers, will ease you in and make it a rewarding pastime. Use thicker yarn for knitting and you will produce yards in no time!

This doesn't have to be solo hobby, either. Join a craft group or knitting circle with like-minded people, where conversation will mingle with the click of knitting needles. You'll get plenty of ideas and advice from other members to encourage you.

Needle Power

Needlecrafts are throwing off their cozy image. An exhibition of "Radical Lace and Subversive Knitting" toured some of the world's top galleries in 2007, while SWAT teams of knitters have been known to turn up in public spaces and craft away as a form of social protest.

Paving the Way

When it rains in urban areas, water has few places to go. It flows away in storm drains toward rivers and streams, but these quickly become overwhelmed in heavy downpours. The earth in gardens and parks can absorb some of that water, but only until it becomes waterlogged.

Anywhere that is paved with concrete—yards, streets, sidewalks and public squares—water has no way of soaking into the ground. Heavy rain is becoming more common as the climate changes, so dealing with the deluge will become more important. Engineers are developing porous road tarmac, but it's not widely used yet.

If you have a patio, path or driveway, choosing the right surfacing materials will create valuable run-off opportunities for rain, slowing the rate at which it reaches fast-flowing rivers and helping to avoid flash flooding.

Permeable paving is key to sustainable urban drainage systems. It is designed to let water trickle through the blocks themselves, or the spaces in between. Permeable concrete or clay blocks, gravel and concrete reinforced grass paving are among the best of these options.

December 1

The World's Deepest Lake

At 5,371 ft, Siberian Lake Baikal is the deepest in the world. Also known as the "Blue Eye of Siberia," it holds more water than all the North American Great Lakes combined.

Despite the harsh environment and five months under ice, Lake Baikal is home to 1,700 species of plants and animals, two-thirds of which are found nowhere else. That's why the giant, banana-shaped lake was declared a UNESCO world heritage site in 1996.

In the face of such an awesome natural wonder, humans seem awfully small. Russian scientists plunged to the depths of the lake only in 2008, and we still have much to learn about its ecosystem. 25 million years after it formed, this special lake is caught in a

constant battle with destructive development. A paper plant on its shore, which discharged waste from the bleaching process, will soon close. Campaigners and politicians opposed placing a major oil pipeline half a mile from the lake and succeeded in altering the route away from its shore.

December 2

Virtual Green

You may be a true nature-lover who, nonetheless, has to spend much of every day chained to a desk in some windowless office to fulfill your work commitments. Even if you are lucky enough to be a park ranger or conservationist full time, the chances are that you too could be inspired by a reminder of other natural treasures beyond your everyday job.

In these winter months, when it is not always as easy to enjoy the great outdoors, why not make your desktop or laptop a constant reminder of the wonders of nature?

If you are a keen photographer, set a beautiful landscape or a detailed insect or plant picture as your computer's wallpaper. Or ask a friend for a copy of a picture you have admired. There are also plenty of generic scenes available for free download online.

Not only will it help you to remember the world beyond the four walls of your study, but your photo might just prompt you to take a break, go out and get a breath of fresh air. If you're in a city, seek out a park to walk in.

December 3

The Bhopal Tragedy

In the early hours of December 3, 1984, while most residents of the central Indian city of Bhopal slept, a cloud of poisonous gas leaked from an American-owned factory. In the days following one of the world's worst ever industrial accidents, 3,000 people died and around 20,000 needed medical treatment for swollen eyes, kidney and liver failure.

Toxic gas had escaped from an underground storage tank at the Union Carbide Corporation's factory, and safety systems at the pesticide plant had failed. Campaigners claim that the accident killed a total of 20,000 people in the aftermath.

Now the factory has been abandoned, but thousands of people live close by in shanty towns, their livestock grazing on the derelict site. Union Carbide denied that toxic material was left behind, but a 2004 investigation found that drinking water nearby was 500 times more toxic than World Health Organization limits.

More than two decades later, the issue of cleaning up and restoring a clean, safe drinking-water supply has yet to be resolved. A settlement was made in compensation for the thousands of victims, but it was far from enough.

December 4

Cotton On

Say "cotton" and thoughts turn to a versatile, soft, natural fabric, a staple of most wardrobes, with a pretty friendly reputation.

Cotton is grown on 3 percent of the world's farming land, but uses a staggering one-quarter of all pesticides. It's a stark reminder that the cost of that plain cotton T-shirt is not simply what's printed on the price tag.

Organic cotton is widely available, but even with fewer chemicals, cotton is a very thirsty crop, lapping up 2.6 percent of all water used on the planet each year.

Cotton is not about to be replaced overnight and it has a lot of advantages over synthetic, petrochemical textiles. But it's worth considering fabrics such as fast-growing bamboo (see January 27 for more information). Try to extend the lifespan of your cotton garments by taking care of them, repairing small tears and passing them on to friends or to charity shops for resale when you can't wear them any more. When it just won't last any longer, try to salvage some for patchwork or cleaning rags, and give to a textile recycler as the last resort.

December 5

Winter Seasonal Foods

Winter may seem like the most difficult time to eat in season, but with a small adjustment in expectations, you can enjoy bountiful fresh produce all through the colder months (see also March 24).

If you have been growing your own vegetables, you can rest on the laurels of a well-stocked larder. While some farmers' markets take a break during the less productive winter months, shoppers can still stock up before they close for the season.

Seasonal foods for December and January include cabbage, parsnips, leeks, shallots, pumpkin, squashes and beetroot. Certain sea food is at its best during the winter months, like sea bass, halibut, lobster, mussels and scallops. February may be the shortest month, but it also has a reputation as the lean month. Undeservedly so, as leeks, early rhubarb, goose and shallots are at their best, as well as many other winter crops.

Plant winter varieties of lettuce and other salad crops for fresh and very local leaves throughout the colder months. Endive, chicory, rocket, spinach, chard and mizuna are all hardy plants that will cope with the cold and can be grown in the ground or pots.

Hybrid Cars

With all the stars driving them, hybrid cars have certainly had their moment in the limelight lately. "Hybrid" means that they combine two sources of fuel, cutting down on the consumption of oil-based fuels and releasing less carbon dioxide. There are a variety of models, including the Prius and Honda shown here, but they usually use a battery to power the car at slow speeds or in stop-start traffic. As an alternative to more traditional vehicles, they definitely offer greater efficiency and produce less pollution.

For some people who must drive many miles, a hybrid makes a significant contribution to cutting the environmental damage of the journey, and the running costs are much lower. But they don't offer totally carbon-free transport. Walking, cycling, public transport or not making the journey at all are greener options.

Hybrids are not quite as green as electric cars, which can, at least in theory, be powered from a renewable energy source. Electric cars must be regularly recharged, and until recharging points are as common as gas stations, they won't be a realistic option for many.

December
7

Do Away with Disposables

Paper napkins have a lot to answer for. Also plastic forks, facial cleansing wipes and disposable cameras. Our grandparents, who knew scarcity, would be horrified that we make so many items to use just once and throw away.

As party season approaches, disposable plates, cups, silverware and napkins seem like a lifesaver—anything to cut down the mountain of dishes! But they are creating a mountain of garbage which is doing no favors for the planet.

Try to cut down on single-use items by serving finger food (no need for a plate), hiring glasses and asking a friend to help with the dishes. When you must use disposables, pick compostable paper rather than plastic or polystyrene. Invest in a set of good quality linen napkins for that special dinner party, then simply put them in the washing machine when you have a little extra space, so they are ready for the next time.

Choose one disposable item that you can replace with a reusable equivalent.

Make Your Holiday Cards

Every year millions of holiday cards arrive in post boxes, bringing seasonal greetings and a little cheer. If you can't bear the thought of electronic greetings (and many websites offer fun, free options), try making your own personalized cards instead of opting for mass-produced ones. Better still, use recycled materials to cut down on waste.

Get creative with odds and ends of wrapping paper or old decorations. If you are a keen photographer and have managed to snap any beautiful wintry scenes, print a small copy onto recycled card. Make templates of simple shapes like a tree, angel, star and holly leaves. Use pieces of wrapping paper, old posters or magazines to cut out the shapes and put together the festive pictures. Add decorations to a simple tree and a bright candle flame with pen, paint or more collage materials. Another winter winner is a snowflake. Choose thin paper or material and cut a round shape. Then fold it in half at least three times, so it is a small cone, and snip a pattern that will be repeated across the flake.

Most cards are too pretty to just appreciate for a few weeks. Make beautiful gift tags for next year by cutting images from this year's cards.

December 9

Worth its Weight in Chocolate

When the Spanish conquistadors arrived in Mexico, they found the Aztecs not only eating and drinking cocoa, but also using cacao beans as currency. So Cortes promptly planted a plantation, not for food but for money—it really does grow on trees!

Although no longer a currency, chocolate is still a genuine treasure. But we need to be careful this treat doesn't damage the environment and exploit the growers. Cortes did quite enough of that!

Make sure to only buy organic, fair-trade chocolate. Organic chocolate will have less environmental impact and fewer of the unpronounceable ingredients often found in regular chocolates. Fair trade means that cacao growers are given a fair price for their beans and have better working conditions. Like coffee, cacao thrives in developing countries where fair trade practices benefit the whole community. Ethical chocolate is better for the environment, the farmers, and your health; now that's a gift for everyone.

Ethical Chocs

❀ Green & Black's
❀ Equal Exchange chocolates
❀ Ithaca Fine Chocolates
❀ Divine Chocolate
❀ Endangered Species Chocolate Company

December 10

Dinosaurs

As well as capturing the imagination of children large and small, dinosaurs and their fossils tell us some incredible things about the planet we call home.

They emerged 230 million years ago, give or take a year or two, and dominated the earth for 160 million years, making them pretty successful creatures (humans have only been around for 200,000 years at most, after all).

Scientists have been able to find out a little about them from fossils and amber (fossilized tree resin), but there is still a great deal of mystery surrounding them.

Dinosaurs were very good at adapting. Living all over the planet for hundreds of millions of years, some evolved to hunt, others to run fast—to escape being eaten by the hunters. The pterosaur was the largest creature ever to fly: with a 36-foot wingspan, it was as large as a glider or light aircraft. Some scientists believe that flying dinosaurs developed into the birds we know today.

But even these adaptable creatures eventually died out. Theories vary as to why, but the possibility of natural disaster or global warming wiping them out might ring alarm bells for us today.

December 11

Water-Efficient Appliances

By now, we all realize that water is a precious resource. After cutting down on water use in the bathroom and tackling waste from dripping taps and leaks, choosing appliances that use water efficiently is the next step.

Machines vary a great deal in the amount of water they use, as well as in energy consumption. The most efficient washing machines use less than half of the water per cycle of the least efficient, for example. Newer machines and front-loaders tend to use much less water, and standards are improving all the time. Researchers at an English university are working on a model that uses just one cup of water, a pinch of detergent and a fraction of the energy of the best currently available models.

When buying a new dishwasher, washing machine, or shower, ask sales staff about water use and inspect labels for information. Ensure that it is properly installed to avoid potential leaks.

It's also worth getting acquainted with the instruction book to find out how you should use it with the most efficient settings.

December 12

Dreaming of a Green Christmas

If your living-room floor looks like the end of the world shortly after the kids attack their presents, you will be all too aware how much trash can be created during Christmas. Add to that the leftovers from the Christmas dinner, discarded gifts and party games, and it's easy to see why the garbage strains under the weight of the holidays. Now is the time to plan ahead for a zero-waste Christmas.

Pick gifts, foods and decorations that have little packaging. Try to pick practical as well as pretty presents; they are more likely to be used and appreciated. Edible presents are a great choice, and you can make them yourself for a personalized gift.

Choose good quality wrapping paper that can be reused, and persuade everyone to open their parcels carefully so that you can save the paper.

It's tempting to buy the whole grocery store for the holidays, but plan an exact shopping list of what you will need for each meal to cut down on food waste, and arm yourself with ideas on cooking up the leftovers. See December 7 for more on reducing party waste.

December 13

Our Closest Relatives

Anyone visiting a zoo cannot fail to notice a family resemblance between the apes and human beings. Whether it's their hands, facial expressions or group behavior, there is plenty of visible evidence to back up the fact that primates are our closest relatives in the animal kingdom.

But sadly, the zoo may soon be the only place to see hundreds of primates under threat of extinction in the wild. Of 634 known species, the International Union for Conservation of Nature has put more than 300 on its "Red List" of endangered animals.

From southern African bushbabies (below) to the massive mountain gorillas (above) of the African Great Lakes, primates are at risk from the destruction of the habitats in which they live, hunting and the illegal trade in wildlife.

Apes have a key role in their natural environment, whether it is dispersing seeds or clearing routes through forests. Often the key to protecting populations of monkeys and apes is conserving the places where they live.

Remarkably, new species are still being discovered, like the 40 different kinds of primate discovered in Madagascar in recent years. Meanwhile, conservation projects are trying to ensure these remarkable animals are still walking the face of the planet with future generations of humans.

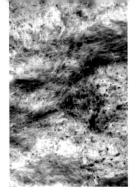

Eco-Economy

Often when you are trying to cut down on the power or materials you use, there's a nice reward for your wallet too. But not always. Some green modifications to our homes involve a hefty investment. There may be several that we want to make, but cannot afford.

Governments and local authorities are slowly waking up to the importance of making it easier (and cheaper) for folk to be green. As well as providing recycling facilities and cycleways, some give grants to homeowners to help with energy-saving investments. These schemes might be limited to certain areas, specific improvements or a small budget, but it's a step in the right direction.

In the UK, one government fund ran out of money in just one hour and 15 minutes, showing just how many people want to be greener if only they were able.

Support for installing renewable energy, efficient boilers (right: a wood-pellet boiler) and insulation (top: rock-wool insulation) is common. In some low-income areas, free energy-saving light bulbs have been given away. Local energy suppliers and charities may also offer help.

December 15

Out with the Old

The stores are bursting at the seams with gifts, and if you are lucky enough to be getting any of them, it might be a good time to clear out some of the old clutter to make way. If there are any parcels under the tree that look suspiciously like books, CDs or DVDs, it's an opportunity to flick through your collection and pass on any that you no longer use.

And if you are picking out a new party dress or plan to hit the January sales, why not go through your wardrobe for old clothes that you don't need any more (see January 3 for an eco-friendly alternative to freshen up your wardrobe).

This time of the year can be particularly tough for families on a tight budget, and there are plenty of local appeals for toys, children's clothes and household goods.

This is also a peak time for charity-shop and thrift-store sales, as people try to pick up vintage or unique presents for their nearest and dearest. So any goods donated will be particularly appreciated during December.

Deck the Halls the Green Way

There are green arguments for and against a real Christmas tree or a fake one. Most real trees are farmed, and therefore replaced. Choose one with roots that can be replanted, and keep it well watered, or get it chipped for composting. A plastic one, on the other hand, may last many years but uses up petro-chemical resources. Whatever you decide, re-use your decorations one year to the next, adding some new home-made baubles if you want to freshen things up. Home-made decorations also make lovely, simple gifts.

See the panel for ideas on ways you can get in the festive mood by making your own.

Make Your Own!

❀ Bake cookies to hang on the tree (best where there are no pets or small children to be tempted!).

❀ Collect holly and evergreen foliage for a festive wreath (an old metal coathanger can be fashioned into a frame).

❀ Sew, knit or patchwork small stockings for the tree and larger ones to hang on a wall or fireplace.

❀ Stick cloves into slices of orange and dry in a warm oven. Tie with red ribbon and add a cinnamon stick for scented, festive heaven.

December 17

Festive Drinks

It wouldn't be Christmas without happy hour for many of us, and why not? It's the holidays, after all. But not all drinks have the same impact on the environment.

The ingredients for a locally made beer may have clocked up 600 miles traveling to the brewery, into the store and, crucially, to your comfy armchair. But buy a multinational's brand, heavily marketed and exported from another country, and the food miles can reach 24,000—the distance around the planet!

The equation is the same with wine. New Zealand white might travel well to California, red may taste lovely in London, but huge amounts of energy are needed to transport that glass of chardonnay halfway across the world to you. Opt for local wine and if you

don't live in an area that supports vineyards, at least cut down the miles by choosing the same continent.

When buying drinks, also think about what they come in. Bottles are easier to recycle than boxes. Recycling glass is good, but bottle deposit schemes mean the bottle is washed and re-used, using much less energy.

Hostess Gifts

It's always nice to bring a gift to the hostess when you are invited to a party, but how do you prevent your offering costing the earth?

A home-made gift might go down well, whether it's a food contribution to the party or a treat to enjoy later. A well-stocked cupboard of jams and jellies comes in very handy here, and freshly baked bread, cookies or cake will hardly be refused! Hand-crafted Christmas decorations or potpourri are also bound to delight.

If you are pressed for time or prefer to buy something, apply the same ethical and environmental standards to your purchases for others as you would to your own shopping. Always buy local and organic, and support the little guy where possible. Locally pressed apple juice, organic wine or a tasty morsel from a neighborhood bakery make lovely party presents, for example.

Dig into your stash of reusable gift bags, or simply use a pretty ribbon rather than gift wrapping the whole item.

December 19

What a Lovely Goat

Only five shopping days until Christmas and still can't think what to buy Uncle Fred?

What about a goat, a swarm of bees or even a teacher?

In recent years, a number of charities have offered "gifts" that, instead of going directly your nearest and dearest, are given on their behalf to a community or family that really needs them.

If your friends have everything they need, it's a great alternative to yet another matching bath set. Or, since they'll miss out on the fun of tearing the paper off that goat, couple it with a small home-made gift. And it works for birthdays and wedding gifts as well.

For the less altruistic, there are plenty of other ways to give a gift without adding yet more clutter at Christmas. Prepare your own gift certificates promising babysitting, gardening or carrying out home repairs or improvements. Or else buy tickets for the movies or the theatre, or for the big game to give something they can look forward to when all the sparkle of the holidays has faded.

December 20

Holiday Flowers

If we balk at the idea of flying green beans halfway around the world, there is no point in doing the same with red roses. Air-freighting, refrigeration, chemicals and pesticides could mean that thoughtful bouquet of blooms leaves your green credentials wilting.

The UK flower market, for example, is dominated by flowers grown in Kenya. They are transported thousands of miles, emitting nearly two tons of CO_2 per ton of flowers.

In the USA, however, ethical, organic flowers are worth more than $8 million a year—demonstrating how many customers care not only for the lucky recipient of the bouquet, but the planet too.

Ask where your florist gets their blooms and encourage local producers where you can find them. Better still, why not buy a flowering pot plant that keeps growing for a gift that keeps on giving? Or make a bouquet from your own garden for a definitively local, chemical-free option.

Fair Flowers Fair Plants is a European organization that campaigns for flowers and plants to be produced in sustainable and ethical ways. Find out more at www.fairflowers-fairplants.com.

December 21

Midwinter

In the dark depths of midwinter, many cultures have sought and found an opportunity to celebrate the moment when days start to lengthen again. The promise of summer, warmth and plenty, though still a long way off, begins to unfold.

In the northern hemisphere, ancient civilizations often worshiped their sun gods at this time of year, relieved that their world would grow no darker. A last great feast would be held, before the coldest part of winter arrived.

Some Stone Age sites are pretty sophisticated when it comes to marking the winter solstice. Stonehenge in England is just one ancient monument aligned according to where sunlight falls at sunset on the winter solstice.

The Romans had a winter festival called Saturnalia, when slaves and masters switched roles. Yule was celebrated by the Germanic peoples in the latter part of December and early January, with singing, eating, drinking and enjoying the heat from burning a yule log. Finnish children enjoy a visit and presents from the Yule Goat or Joulupukki, a Father Christmas figure. Many of the traditions from these pre-Christian events were later absorbed into Christmas.

Pull the Plug

We're often oblivious to the power used by all our electronic devices when they are switched on, but many continue to quietly gobble up electricity when we aren't even using them.

Cell phone chargers left plugged in turn just 5 per cent of the energy they use into phone power. The other 95 per cent is completely wasted (if your charger feels warm when it's not in use, you know it's still consuming energy).

Leaving televisions and computers on "stand-by" can lead you to think that they are inactive, but they keep using up expensive, carbon-emitted power.

The average house has around 12 gadgets on stand-by or charging at any one time. Check your own home – devices like stereos, DVD players, TVs, games consoles, satellite and cable boxes and MP3 chargers use plenty of energy when not in use if they are not turned off properly.

Smart plugs are now available which switch off devices left on stand-by after a certain time. But getting in the habit of turning things off and unplugging chargers when not in use is just as effective.

December 23

Festive Table Decorations

An elegant placeholder can set off the Christmas table beautifully, and if your holiday table mixes people who sometimes clash, you can seat them at opposite ends. But there's no need to buy an expensive set when you can make your own sustainable alternatives. If you have too much on your plate, ask a friend or child to take on this creative task.

Use something organic—a holly leaf, orange, or pine cone—as a starting point. Write names on the item or attach a small card.

For something a little more fancy, use leftover bits of wrapping paper to wrap a chocolate or small gift for each guest, attaching a name tag to the ribbon. Or place a small candle at each place setting, taping a name around each one.

For simple, recycled napkin rings, cut inch-long lengths of a cardboard tube (the kind that comes in the middle of paper towels) and paint or cover in colored paper to match the tablecloth. Or tie a small sprig of winter greenery around each napkin. You could attach a name card to either type for a combined napkin and placeholder. Or just decorate your table festively!

December 24

Kiss Me, I'm Green!

Ah, it wouldn't be Christmas without the opportunity to kiss handsome strangers!

Strange to think that mistletoe, this most romantic of plants, is poisonous and technically a parasite, growing on the branches of other host trees or shrubs. That doesn't sound too good, but it plays an essential part in its environment, as a food source and even nesting sites for certain bird species.

Mistletoe has been a common Christmas decoration for two hundred years. It is not meant to touch the ground between harvesting and hanging, preferably above a doorway for the whole year to protect the house from fires. The tradition of kissing under it comes from Scandinavia, where enemies who encountered one another beneath mistletoe had to maintain a truce for a day.

Along with holly and ivy, mistletoe is a reminder of how our traditions are bound up with nature's seasons. And they all make much prettier and less destructive decorations than plastic baubles with toxic paints. Only ever take a tiny amount of what you find, so they are there to enjoy for many future celebrants.

December 25

Christmas Day

Hopefully, Christmas Day is an opportunity to relax and not expend too much of your personal energy resources, but with the family home all day and everyone giving their new toys a whirl, it's easy to get through plenty of electricity. Here are some energy-saving tips for the big day:

LED Christmas lights use one-tenth of the power of the regular kind. Save the Christmas lights for after dark, when they can be seen properly anyway, and turn on fewer room lights so that the tree stands out. Don't forget to turn off all the Christmas lights when you go out or to bed (they can be a fire hazard, too).

Plan how you will cook the Christmas meal to make best use of your oven space, and don't forget to turn the stove off when you've finished.

Don't leave the fridge or freezer door open while preparing food. If it's full, put bottles in a bucket of cool water outside for natural, energy-efficient refrigeration.

Stock up on rechargeables, ready for any new battery-powered toys or gadgets. And try candles instead of lights.

Leftovers

Few households are without plenty of leftovers after a big holiday dinner. But with a little planning, you can use what's left for tasty, low-effort meals in the days to come. Plan to bake some delicious bread and make soups, or keep leftover meat and cheese for sandwiches and light lunches.

If you had poultry, pick all the meat off the bones to use in sandwiches, pies and curry dishes. Boil up the bones and scraps from turkey, chicken or ham for stock. Just add to sauteed onions and vegetables and simmer for a half hour for a warming winter broth.

An excess of boiled, mashed or roast potatoes will make a tasty day-after breakfast, especially if well seasoned and fried up with leftover cabbage, carrot or parsnips.

If you have guests who are traveling home after the big day, pack them a hearty lunch.

If you didn't cook a big dinner and have no leftovers to worry about, why not see if you can volunteer at a soup kitchen and join in with others to provide a meal for someone in need?

December 27

Think Positive

We are bombarded by statistics, science and warnings about the environment—how many years we have before climate change is irreversible, how fast sea levels will rise, the number of species being lost. It is daunting and difficult to work out what's happening, never mind address this future mapped out by newspapers and green groups.

There are good news stories too—of conservation projects already protecting areas of forest and wetland and the species that live in them, of pollution curbed and cleaned up.

It is clearly important to engage with environmental issues and become better informed about what we can do. There is plenty to worry about, but as we prepare to welcome the New Year, let's inhale a breath of optimism about the positive impact we can have. Reflect on the changes you have made in your own life in the past year.

Having a vision of where we want go helps to keep us going—living in harmony with a thriving environment, where waste and pollution are things of the past and there's enough to go around for everyone.

December 28

Laundry List

Of course you want clean, fresh clothes, but do they really need to be the brightest, whitest, softest fabrics on the block? Probably not at the expense of even more toxic chemicals in your home and flushed down the drain.

When picking out detergent, try to look beyond the impressive claims of leading brands. Check the ingredients: phosphates, phosphonates and carboxylates should ring alarm bells. There are a number of eco-brands on the market that are worth trying. They harness the power of vegetable-based soaps rather than petrochemical-based cleaners.

For clothes that need a little extra cleaning, soak beforehand or dab with a little undiluted detergent or lemon juice.

Some eco-warriors dispense with using commercial washing powder altogether, using lemon juice or soap flakes instead.

Others swear by special washing balls that go into the machine with the clothes and clean by agitating them during the cycle.

Don't forget to try to fill the machine, run it at a cooler temperature and use an eco-setting for greater efficiency. If you're looking for a new machine or other laundry tips, see the panel on January 2.

December 29

As the Year Ends...

It's that time for reflecting on the year that has almost passed and considering how we want to enhance our lives in the approaching one.

Hopefully it's been a year of striving to be greener, and a revelation that doing so isn't a chore but a better way of living for ourselves, our families and our communities. If every reader kept up just half of the practical suggestions in this book, we could really start to make a difference!

By now, you will have a sense of what changes are most difficult for you and where your gifts naturally lie. Perhaps you are brilliant at crafts and can give old materials a new lease of life. Maybe you are very persuasive and can help others see where they can make

changes too. Others will hate preaching or find it impossible to make time to cook from scratch or prepare home-made gifts. That's OK—it's not about changing the world all by ourselves.

Pass on this book to a friend who might like to do more for the environment and share discoveries you have found useful with others.

December 30

Another Year of Tips

If you have found it useful to have regular ideas for greening your lifestyle, you could sign up to an email list to keep them coming through the forthcoming year.

A regular message landing in your inbox will give you a steady supply of tips and pointers. Checking in with your favorite green blogs will help take the slog out of doing your part, by reminding you there are lots of others out there trying their best too.

Connect with a virtual or real community that best reflects your interests and talents—whether it's an organic gardening club or a mailing list with recycled crafts for children. If organic food whets your appetite, try the Soil Association's monthly email from www.whyorganic.org. If you are a born campaigner, there are plenty of local, national and international groups out there. Find one which is working on the issues you care most about—whether protecting wildlife, cutting pollution or improving cycle routes. Other general websites like Mother Earth News let you choose updates on energy, gardening, self-sufficiency and more, at www.motherearthnews.com.

December 31

Wow, What a World!

From the high peaks of Nepal's Himalayas to the unexplored depths of the Pacific Ocean rifts, our planet is spectacular, even if we know only a small slice.

Few of us will ever live on the frozen surface of Antarctica or in the arid Sahara desert, and yet these harsh landscapes can support plant, animal and occasionally even human life.

The variety of species is mind-boggling, from hungry fly-catcher plants to the giant, ancient redwoods; from tiny, spotted ladybugs in the garden to the great African elephants of the savannah.

And this complexity helps life endure in all its richness. Humans have all too often sought to exploit the wealth of nature. It's clear that living within our natural means and in harmony with the environment, rather than exploiting it, is a much more enriching way.

It's been a pleasure spending the year with you, as we all try to do our part! And as we turn over a new leaf again for the new year, remember: we're all worth it.

If you like a glass of bubbly to ring in the New Year, why not hunt out a local fizz?

In the bleak mid-winter
Frosty wind made moan,
Earth stood hard as iron,
Water like a stone;
Snow had fallen, snow on snow,
Snow on snow,
In the bleak mid-winter,
Long ago.

—Christina Rossetti

INDEX

Aborigines (Australia) 124, 248
aerosols 201
agriculture: 192, 359; chickens
  183; fair trade 76; free range 63;
  genetic modification 199, 254;
  monocultures 61; organic 23,
  130, 209, 230; pesticides 199;
  sustainable 14, 76, 199
air conditioning 178
animals: amphibians 112, 313; big
  cats 333; dinosaurs 30, 371;
  endangered species 24, 61, 194,
  220, 255, 374; farm animals 62,
  209; frogs 19, 112, 313; invasive
  species 355; "new" species 258;
  owls 262; pandas 255; penguins
  138; pets 217, 240; polar bears
  127; primates 374; red squirrels
  19; sharks 293; tropical cone
  snails 220; whales 13, 70; World
  Animal Day 303
asparagus 126
Australia 53, 67, 124, 133, 197,
  230, 248, 258

baking soda 82, 143, 318
banking 341
bartering 208, 323
batteries 27, 324, 386
berries 213, 219

birds: bird feeder 299; endangered
  birds 91, 271; migration 53, 157;
  owls 262; penguins 138
biodiversity 18, 19, 112, 165
Brazil 24
bread 33
buildings 131, 141, 294; green
  roof 203; retro-fitting 131; World
  Heritage Day 131
butterflies 66
Buy Nothing Day 357

California 7, 19
Cameroon 180
camping 222
Canada 30, 168, 179, 280
carbon emissions 20, 37, 47, 55,
  60, 67, 73, 77, 121, 153, 171,
  178, 190, 205, 243, 291, 310,
  319, 367; *see also* energy: conservation
carbon footprint, calculating 47
carbon offsets 190
cars 146, 290, 319, 367
chickens 183
China 255
chocolate 370
Christmas 386: cards 25, 369;
  decorations 377, 384, 385;
  drinks 378; gifts 373, 387;

One World Week 321
owls 262
ozone 285

packaging 29, 64, 176, 261, 265
paint 234
palm oil 61
pandas 255
paper: books 45; cardboard 305; envelopes 88; giftwrap 288; junk mail 301; magazines 43; newspaper 43; printing 218; recycling 43; work 134
peat bogs 34
penguins 138
pesticides 200
Petra (Jordan) 248
photography 214
plants: algae 340; bamboo 46; cotton 365; flowers 309, 381; green roof 203; lavender 233; lawn 245; medicine 40, 79, 174; natural dyes 276; pollination 228; seaweed 108; tea trees 40; willow 174
plastic: bags 42, 265; bottles 168; recycling 274; reusing 206
pollution: 12, 69; air 179, 201, 241; carbon offsets 190; Clean Air Day 179; Clean Up the World Weekend 283; nuclear 139; water 364
polar bears 127
Pollinator Week 228

population growth 216
potato chips 256
potatoes 335

rainforests 79, 325, 344
recycling: 56, 119, 227, 263, 346; batteries 324; cans 169; CDs and DVDs 128; computers 231; cycles 85; freecycle 72; glass 188; glasses 195; pens 272; plastic 274; scrap metal 251
renewable energy 16, 282: biofuels 61, 90; geothermal 347; Isle of Eigg 198; microgeneration 171; solar power 27, 137, 205; wave power 107; wind power 87
resolutions 20
rice 14, 199

schools: 116, 260; air quality 241; Florence Brown Project 250; transportation 260, 300
scoop shops 176
Scotland 85, 97, 198, 224
shopping: 147, 160; Buy Nothing Day 357; Compacters 338; food 189, 236, 289; Green Consumer Day 297
simple living 80, 97, 129, 202, 255, 264, 277, 298
sharks 293
Slow Food 345
Sri Lanka 24
swimming 249

ACKNOWLEDGEMENTS

The publisher would like to thank the following people for their help in the preparation of this book: Sara Myers for editorial assistance, photo research and the index; Chloe van Grieken for picture research and graphic design assistance; Ewan Stevenson for editorial assistance; and Wendy Brawer, Duncan Broomhead, Rebecca Pyne, Anna Roebuck and Debbie White.

Photograph Credits

The publisher would like to thank the photographers and libraries for permission to reproduce images in this book. The RSA WEEE man (page 26), designed by Paul Bonomini, is reproduced by courtesy of RSA (photographer David Ramkalawon). The Green Map® icons (page 32) are © copyright Green Map System, Inc., 2008. All other photographs are © Jupiter Images, except those listed below, by page number. Every effort has been made to credit the author of these images, but if we have made any errors, we apologise. Please notify Saraband with any errors so that we can correct any future editions.

© Lars Aronsson 357b; © Duncan Broomhead 144b; © Tomas Castelazo 332b; Evstaviev 139b; Follash 294b; Luca Frediani 364b; Leonard G 345b; Liftarn 367b; © Clare Haworth-Maden 110b; © Nick Hayes 299b; © Sara Hunt 23t, 59b, 62b, 68b, 97 (both), 98b, 100t, 102b, 109b, 130b, 136t, 149t, 183t, 186b, 204t, 210b, 217t, 219 (both), 240b, 244b, 343t, 369b, 384b; Ewig Lernender 343b; Martin 332t; NASA: 51; NIGMS, photograph by Kerry Matz 220; © John O'Neill 66t, 80b, 103b, 113, 130t, 175, 193b; © Anna Roebuck 206 (both); Sansculotte 362t; US Department of Defense 337 (both); USDA 355b; ©Debbie White 23b, 81, 177b, 186t.